My Dearest Mouse

My Dearest Mouse
'The Wind in the Willows' letters

Kenneth Grahame

Introduction by David Gooderson
Published in association with The Bodleian Library

PAVILION
MICHAEL JOSEPH

First published in Great Britain in 1988 by
Pavilion Books Limited
196 Shaftesbury Avenue, London WC2H 8JL
in association with Michael Joseph Limited
27 Wrights Lane, Kensington, London W8 5TZ

Letters and Ernest H. Shepard line illustrations
© The Dorneywood Trust
Illustration p 6 © BBC Hulton Picture Library
Illustrations pp 7, 40, 88 © H & B Graeme, Fowey
Illustrations pp 10, 24, 172 © Bodleian Library
Illustration p 14 © Iona Opie/Bodleian Library
Illustration p 18 © The Royal Institution of
Cornwall
Illustrations pp 30, 34, 56, 110 © Barbara
Edwards

Editor: Marilyn Watts
Associate editor: Russell Ash
Designed by Kevin Shenton

British Library Cataloguing in Publication Data
Grahame, Kenneth
My dearest mouse: 'The wind in the willows'
letters.
1. Grahame, Kenneth—Biography
2. Authors, Scottish—Biography
I. Title
823'.8   PR4727

ISBN 1 85145 154 4

Phototypeset by Tradespools Ltd, Frome, Somerset
Colour separation by C.L.G., Verona, Italy
Printed in Great Britain by Hazell, Watson &
Viney Ltd, Aylesbury, Bucks

INTRODUCTION

In 1899 Kenneth Grahame was Secretary of the Bank of England and the distinguished author of two volumes of stories about children, *The Golden Age* (1895) and *Dream Days* (1898). He was forty, and a confirmed bachelor. Yet in June of that year, after a brief courtship conducted mainly by post, he married Elspeth Thomson. At thirty-six she had published a penny novelette, *Amelia Jane's Ambition*, and was renowned for the luncheons and soirées at which she entertained personalities from the world of literature and art. It was an unlikely match. Like Badger, Grahame loved solitude and hated 'company' whereas Elspeth thrived on it. Like Mole he was shy and retiring, while she was forthright and garrulous. And although undoubtedly 'as nice as his books' he failed to satisfy her physical expectations. Shortly before the marriage he had confided to a friend:

> 'My beastly virtue has been my enemy through life, but once married I will try and be frankly depraved, and all will go well.'

It did not. While still on honeymoon in Cornwall, Elspeth sent a cry for help to Thomas Hardy's first wife, Emma, whose reply was most discouraging:

> 'I can scarcely think that love proper, and enduring, is in the nature of men...theirs being akin to children's, a sort of easy affectionateness...keeping separate a good deal is a wise plan in crises.'

On 12 May, 1900, the Grahame's only child was born prematurely. 'A big fellow', partially blind, he was christened Alastair and nicknamed

Portrait of Kenneth Grahame.

Fowey Church. The Grahames were married here in 1899.

'Mouse', and at once became the focus for his parents' thwarted emotions. Grahame himself had never wanted to grow up and once said:

> 'I feel I should never be surprised to meet myself as I was when a little chap of five, suddenly coming round a corner...the queer thing is, I can remember everything I felt then, the part of my brain I used from four till about seven can never have altered.'

When Mouse reached the age of four, Grahame began to identify with him in a way untypical of Edwardian fathers, and for the next three

Miniature portrait of Alastair Grahame,
aged about four years.

years their relationship was at its closest. The nightly bedtime story was of ritual importance. On the evening of Mouse's fourth birthday, Grahame wrote:

> 'He had a bad crying fit . . . and I had to tell him stories about moles, giraffes and water-rats (he selected these as subjects) till after 12.'

That same month the Grahames were late for a dinner engagement. Elspeth, who was ready and getting agitated, summoned the maid and demanded to know where her husband was. The maid replied:

> 'He's with Master Mouse, Madam; he's telling him some ditty [story] or other about a Toad.'

Marriage and motherhood were placing an increasing strain on Elspeth's nerves. She would sometimes spend most of the day on a sofa sipping hot water. Shortly after Mouse's fourth birthday she went away to Woodhall Spa in Lincolnshire for a prolonged rest-cure, but nevertheless wrote to Grahame twice and sometimes three times a day, eager to know how he and Mouse were and asking what tips she should give to the hotel servants. He replied, less frequently, in the same mis-spelt baby talk he had used in his courtship letters and in one letter gave a detailed picture of his 'larks' with Mouse in nearby Kensington Gardens. Eyebrows must have been raised at the sight of the tall City man practising 'yumpy-yumps' on the steps of the Albert Memorial, after which he had a 'well-earned' cigarette. Later that afternoon, tea was taken under a tree, and when Mouse's mouth was 'well-stuffed' with bread and butter, he said softly, 'Now tell me about this mole'. Grahame had to spin out the mole story for the 'ole of tea-time', and added:

> 'There was a tauly [story] in which a mole, a badger and a water-rat was characters and I got them terribly mixed up as I went along, but ee always stratened em out and remembered wich was wich.'

Mouse's appetite for stories was voracious. He was always wanting to know 'what the mole and water-rat did annuvver day'. Sometimes Grahame managed to escape, reporting that, 'We went to tea and mercifully I didn't ave to tell no taulid [stories]'. On other occasions Mouse would 'annexe' the housekeeper, Mrs Blunt. Grahame wrote that she returned 'as we all do – pale and exhausted with effort'.

In her short memoir, *First Whisper of 'The Wind in the Willows'* (1944), Elspeth depicts her son as the angelic 'Listener' drinking in enchantment from 'the Story-Teller'. But there was another side to Mouse's character which was less appealing. Once, when he wanted to see his father, who was in the bath at the time, he tried to break down the door; if 'Dutchy' (his German governess) crossed him, he was liable to kick her 'about the body'. And he was the terror of Kensington Gardens. He kicked and slapped little girls, digging 'ten fingers deep into their tender flesh'. According to 'Dutchy', the Keepers made an official complaint to the Office of HM Works, and members of the public threatened to intervene.

Grahame merely asked him why he did it – Mouse replied that he had 'a leaning' that way – and only reported to Elspeth any lapses of affection towards himself:

> 'Left im at Broad Walk, ee avin fafely promitt wave ankchiff – but before I get 100 yds I perceive serious difficulties tween im and the German forces – larst I sor of him he sullenly retiring in good order before enemy – but no thought of ankchiff waving or other frivolities.'

the sofa is at the station

A. Grahame

miss stott

Alastair Grahame's portrait of his governess, Miss Stott.

Grahame may have been unconcerned about Mouse's violence, but he took a poor view of his tendency to exult in his exploits, and the story of 'Mr Toad' was developed with gently satirical intent. Mouse loved it. In May, shortly before his seventh birthday, he refused point-blank to go on holiday to Littlehampton with his new nursery governess ('Dutchy' had been replaced by Miss Naomi Stott), because he would miss the adventures of Toad. He was persuaded only by his father's promise that further instalments would be sent by post, and so the letters began.

Having read the letters aloud to Mouse, Miss Stott had the foresight to preserve them and, before leaving Littlehampton, posted them to Elspeth for safe keeping, 'knowing full well', wrote Elspeth, 'that if restored to the author, they would merely be consigned to the waste-paper basket'.

It was now 1907; Grahame had produced nothing since *Dream Days* nine years previously, and certainly had no intention of having the story published. A catalyst was needed. It is ironic that in the case of so male a masterpiece the catalyst should have been a feminist who drove a motor-car.

Constance Smedley had written *Woman: A Few Shrieks!* earlier that year, and among her many other activities she was the European representative of the American magazine, *Everybody's*. The editor had urged her to try to tempt Grahame back into print: she was living at Bray near Cookham Dene, where the Grahames had a house, and she wrote asking him for an appointment. In her autobiography, *Crusaders*, she described their meeting:

> 'I drove over one day in late summer when the mists of early autumn were invading hedge and lane ... Mr. Grahame seemed as remote and shadowy as the countryside; he was encased in the defensiveness which dreads coercion; about him was that peculiar English aroma of dogs, ploughed fields and firelit libraries ... But Mr. Grahame refused all entreaties ... He hated writing; it was physical torture. Why should he undergo it?'

Undaunted, she made friends with Mouse and Elspeth, and their acquaintance 'quickly ripened'. She was invited to dinner on a number of occasions, and soon her patience was rewarded.

It was Elspeth's idea to use the letters as the starting-point for a book. According to Miss Smedley, Mouse was thrilled at the suggestion and was 'the only person who could have persuaded Mr. Grahame into so hated a task'. It must also have helped that part of the story was already more or less in manuscript form.

Once committed, Grahame worked with rare energy. The letters, which he expanded but did not substantially alter, account for little more than a third of *The Wind in the Willows*: they contain a fragment of Chapter 6, and the bulk of Chapters 8, 10, 11 and 12.

In his search for new material, Grahame delved into earlier bedtime stories, particularly those about 'The Mole and the Water Rat', which was his original title for the book. Miss Stott was commandeered to jog Mouse's memory and note down what he told her. In one such note she describes the arrival of Mole and Rat 'at Badger Hall in the Wild Wood', and an encounter with a grumpy housekeeper which was omitted in the book. She suggests to Grahame that: 'If you could tell me any leading questions, I might casually be able to extract more'.

And consciously or subconsciously, as he worked, Grahame began to use the book as an opportunity to express all that had lain dormant for the last nine years. He believed that:

> 'A theme, a thesis, a subject, is in most cases little more than a sort of clothes-line, on which one pegs a string of ideas, quotations, and so on, one's mental undergarments of all shapes and sizes, some possibly fairly new; but most rather old and patched; and they dance and sway in the breeze, and flap and flutter, or hang limp and lifeless; and some are ordinary enough; and some are of a rather private and intimate shape, and rather give the owner away, and show up his or her peculiarities. And owing to the invisible clothes-line they seem to have some connection and continuity.'

The last two 'stories' which Grahame added are the magnificent chapters, 'The Piper at the Gates of Dawn' and 'Wayfarers All'. Straying far from the bedtime story, he returned to the lyrical style of his earlier essays to voice his deepest longings and most profound imaginings.

The eagerly awaited manuscript was sent across the Atlantic to *Everybody's* in the autumn of 1907. It was rejected. The editor was expecting something *about* children, like the earlier Grahame successes, not *for* them – and certainly not about animals.

The indefatigable Miss Smedley then arranged a meeting with the agent, Curtis Brown, who later wrote:

> 'I read it excitedly. It was lovely. I tried it with magazine editors all over England and America. They thought it too fantastic and wouldn't have it.'

Eventually, after 'labouring long and hard', he persuaded Algernon

Studio portrait of Alastair Grahame by Richard Speaight.

Kenneth Grahame's dedication in Alastair Grahame's
copy of *The Wind in the Willows*.

Methuen to publish it, but Methuen did not have sufficient faith in the book to guarantee an advance payment. Brown did, however, secure 'excellent rising royalties, in case the book *should* fulfil my dreams'.

Grahame was urged to find a better title than 'Mr Mole and His Mates', which at the time he considered 'the most practical'. His friend, the artist and playwright Graham Robertson, sent him a list of possibles:

'"Down Stream", "With the Stream", "Among the Sedges", "The Garden of Pan" – no good. It *may* come, as you say, while shaving.'

Methuen advertised it as 'The Wind in the Reeds', which was the original title of the chapter, 'The Piper at the Gates of Dawn'. But when it was realized that this was uncomfortably close to the title of a collection of poems by Yeats, Grahame changed it to *The Wind in the Willows*.

The book was published in England in October, 1908, and later the same year by Charles Scribner in America – thanks largely to the personal recommendation of the then President, Theodore Roosevelt. Family and friends were nervous of the reception the book might get. Elspeth begged her friend Thomas Anstey Guthrie, the F. Anstey who had written *Vice Versa*, to review it, but he declined. Robertson advised Grahame to ask Methuen in his preliminary announcement to state clearly that the book was 'not a political skit, or an Allegory of the Soul...or a social satire'.

As feared, the critics were bewildered and on the whole disapproving.

Punch dismissed it as 'a sort of irresponsible holiday story'. *The Times* concluded that 'as a contribution to natural history the work is negligible'. Only Arnold Bennett and Richard Middleton found it 'entirely successful'. In any event, the public made up its own mind. A second edition appeared the same month and *The Wind in the Willows* soon became an international best seller. Middleton, writing in *Vanity Fair*, echoed the views of countless readers:

> 'When all is said the boastful, unstable Toad, the hospitable Water Rat, the shy, wise, childlike Badger, and the Mole with his pleasant habit of brave boyish impulse, are neither animals nor men, but are types of that deeper humanity which sways us all.'

And a year later, Middleton concluded an article on 'Children's Literature' with:

> 'I should like again to register my opinion that the best book ever written for children and one of the best books ever written for grown-up people is *The Wind in the Willows* by Mr. Kenneth Grahame.'

DAVID GOODERSON
London, 1987

*Where the original letter is unclear, a transcript of
the text is provided on the facing page.
Square brackets in the transcript denote alterations
made by Kenneth Grahame to the manuscript.
Illustrations facing the letters are by Ernest Shepard
unless attributed otherwise.*

THE LETTERS

Green Bank Hotel, Falmouth.

Green Bank Hotel, Cornwall
10 May 1907

This was the Grahame's first visit to Cornwall since their honeymoon.
Patrick Chalmers, in a biography published the year after Grahame's
death, suggests that the parents were not with Mouse at Littlehampton
because they were 'bound to the Bank of England' and, curiously,
misquotes the address of this letter. In fact, as Grahame later wrote, it
was simply that their taste in places was different. Grahame disliked
Littlehampton ('a rather horrid little place') and had loved Cornwall ever
since his first visit to the Lizard in 1884. He wrote of 'the wildness,
freshness and strangeness . . . its grandeur and sparkling air . . . and the
simple, friendly people.'

GREEN BANK HOTEL,
FALMOUTH,
10th May 1907.

My darling Mouse

This is a birthday letter,
to wish you very many happy returns
of the day. I wish we could have
been all together, but we shall
meet again soon, & then we will
have treats. I have sent you two
picture-books, one about Brer
Rabbit, from Daddy, & one about
some other animals, from Mummy,
and we have sent you a boat,

Green Bank Hotel, Cornwall
10 May 1907

The story is already in full swing, with Toad a familiar character. This is a further instalment of the nightly bedtime story which Mouse was so eager not to miss. The brigands and the ransom note do not appear in *The Wind in the Willows*, but once Toad escapes from the window we are in the middle of Chapter 6: 'Mr Toad', where:

> 'tying one end of the improvised rope round the central mullion of the handsome Tudor window which formed such a feature of his bedroom, he scrambled out, slid lightly to the ground, and, taking the opposite direction to the Rat, marched off lightheartedly, whistling a merry tune.'

In the book Grahame omits 'Buggleton' (presumably invented) but keeps the name of the hotel, which may have been suggested by the old Red Lion at Bourne End, just across the river from Cookham in Berkshire, where the Grahames had a house.

painted red, with mast & sails, to sail in the round pond by the windmill — & mummy has sent you a boat-hook to catch it when it comes to shore. Also mummy has sent you some sand-toys to play in the sand with, and a card-game.

Have you heard about the Toad? He was never taken prisoner by brigands at all. It was all a horrid low trick of his. He wrote that letter himself — the letter saying that a hundred pounds must be put in the hollow tree. And he got out of the window early one morning, & went off to a town called Buggleton & went to the Red Lion Hotel & there he found a party that had just motored down from London, & while they were having breakfast he

Green Bank Hotel, Cornwall
10 May 1907

For Grahame, as for many of his contemporaries, the Horseless Carriage –
that 'petrol-piddling monster' as Kipling called it – summed up all that
was worst about so-called 'progress'. Motor-cars were noisy, dirty and
dangerous. Yet for Toad they were the newest craze:

> 'The *real* way to travel! The *only* way to travel! Here to-day – in next week
> to-morrow! Villages skipped, towns and cities jumped – always somebody
> else's horizon! O bliss! O poop-poop!'

went into the stable-yard & found their motor-car & went off in it without even saying Poop-poop! And now he has vanished & every one is looking for him, including the police. I fear he is a bad low animal.

Goodbye, from

Your loving Daddy.

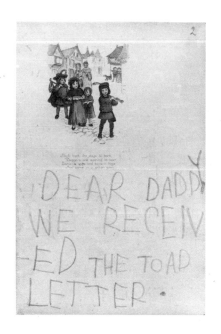

DEAR DADDY
WE RECEIV
-ED THE TOAD
LETTER.

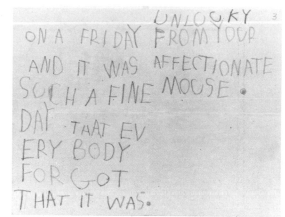

UNLOCKY
ON A FRIDAY FROM YOUR
AND IT WAS AFFECTIONATE
SUCH A FINE MOOSE.
DAY. THAT EV
ERY BODY
FORGOT
THAT IT WAS.

Letter from Alastair Grahame to his father.

Green Bank Hotel, Cornwall
23 May 1907

None of the surviving letters from Littlehampton are 'full of news', but in one Mouse announces: 'I like it here. More witches. More black cats and more broom sticks. And the fairies say they are too busy to come so we shall have to manage by ourselves. With love from Mouse.' On the back of the letter Miss Stott, his governess, adds: 'Mouse says that I am to fill up his letter. We are both enjoying ourselves here and when the weather is warm, we hope to go on the river again.'

GREEN BANK HOTEL,
FALMOUTH.
23rd May 1907.

My dearest Mouse

Thank you very much
for your nice letter. It was very
interesting & full of news, and I
read it through several times.
I hope you have got some warm
weather again by this time. It is
very hard to live in sight of a
beach & not be able to dig, & dig
& dig & dig — all day long.
No doubt you have met some
of the animals & have heard
about Toad's Adventures since
he was dragged off to prison

'O unhappy and forsaken Toad!'
A Nancy Barnhart illustration for *The Wind in the Willows* (1922).

This letter, and the one that follows it, cover the events later described in Chapter 8: 'Toad's Adventures', of *The Wind in the Willows*.

'Forsaken', the pencilled alteration, was added by Grahame at a later date, presumably when re-reading the letters with a view to writing the book. Such alterations are more frequent in the later letters.

by the bobby & the constable. At first
he lay full length on the floor, and
shed bitter tears, and abandoned
himself to dark despair. For he
said "How can I ever hope to be
set free again, I who have been
imprisoned – and justly – so
often, for stealing so many – so
many —— he could not utter the
word, for his sobs choked him.
Base animal that I am (he said);
O unhappy & abandoned toad (he said);
I must languish in this dungeon
(he said) till people have forgotten
the very name of Mr Toad. With
lamentations such as these he
passed his days & nights, refusing
consolation, refusing food or other
light refreshments; till one day

Green Bank Hotel, Cornwall
23 May 1907

As so often in the book, Grahame takes the raw material of the letters and embroiders:

> 'The smell of that buttered toast simply talked to Toad, and with no uncertain voice; talked of warm kitchens, of breakfasts and bright frosty mornings, of cosy parlour firesides on winter evenings, when one's ramble was over and slippered feet were propped on the fender; of the purring of contented cats, and the twitter of sleepy canaries.'

the gaoler's daughter, who was a
tender-hearted young woman, took
pity on him & said 'Cheer up, Toad!
& try & eat a bit of dinner'. But the toad
lay on the floor & wailed & wouldn't
eat his dinner. Then the gaoler's
daughter went & fetched a cup of
hot tea & some very hot buttered
toast, cut thick, very brown on
both sides, with the butter running
through the holes in it in great
golden drops like honey. When
the toad smelt the buttered toast he
sat up & dried his eyes, for he was
exceedingly fond of buttered toast;
& the gaoler's daughter comforted
him & he drank his tea & had
another plate of toast. Then they
discussed plans for his escape from
the dungeon, & the gaoler's daughter

'She arranged the shawl.'
An Arthur Rackham illustration for
The Wind in the Willows (1940).

When in the book the gaoler's daughter says she has an aunt who is a washerwoman, Toad retorts: 'Never mind, think no more about it. I have several aunts who *ought* to be washerwomen.' Grahame took a dim view of relatives, especially aunts and uncles. He satirized them in *The Golden Age* and *Dream Days*, and in an early essay entitled 'Justifiable Homicide', argued humorously for their extinction.

In the book, Grahame omits the violent incident when Toad, disguised as a washerwoman, is beaten by the gaoler. Instead Toad merely has to counter 'chaff and humorous sallies'. He keeps his temper and does his best 'not to overstep the limits of good taste'.

said "Tomorrow my aunt, who is
the washerwoman to the prison,
will bring home your week's washing.
& I will dress you up in her clothes
& you will escape as the washerwoman"
So when the washerwoman came with
the linen, they dressed toad up in
her clothes & put a bonnet on his
head, & out he marched, past the
gaolers, as bold as you please.
As he was passing one of them, the
man said "Hullo mother washerwoman,
why didn't you send home my
Sunday shirt last week, you lazy
old pig?" & he took his stick & beat
her full sore. And the toad was
mad with rage, because he wanted
to give him a punch in the eye,
but he controlled himself, & ran on
through the door, which banged behind
him & he was Free. This is as far as
I have read at present.
Your affectionate
Daddy.

Fowey Hotel, Cornwall
28 May 1907

By moving to the Fowey Hotel, the Grahames were returning to familiar territory. Grahame himself had first discovered Fowey when convalescing from a serious illness in 1899, and was at once captivated by the place, where 'the sea has all the blues in the world and a few over'. It was from the Fowey Hotel that he wrote, and eventually proposed, to Elspeth in letters of lyrical baby-talk. They were married in Fowey and spent most of their honeymoon at the Fowey Hotel.

While in the letters Grahame describes Toad's desperate plight, in the book he again lowers the dramatic temperature. Instead of being lonely and frightened, Toad emerges from prison 'dizzy with the easy success of his daring exploit', as E. H. Shepard's drawing jauntily conveys.

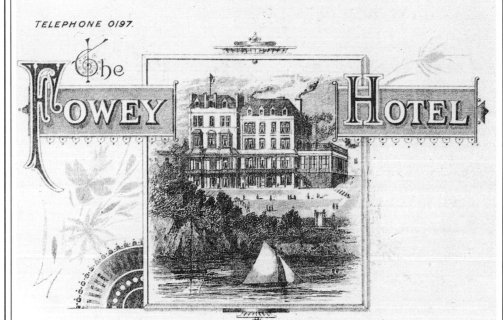

TELEPHONE 0197.

The FOWEY HOTEL

FOWEY, CORNWALL, 28 May 1907.

My dearest Mouse

I am very glad to hear that
you have got rid of your cold, & have
been able to sail your boat in the
pond. Now I daresay you will want
to hear something more of the sad
misadventures of Mr. Toad. Well,
when he found himself outside the
prison gates it was quite dark &
he was in a strange land, with no
no friends, & he was frightened, &
didn't know what to do. But he

'Stand away from the window.'
An Arthur Rackham illustration for
The Wind in the Willows (1940).

Toad's horror at losing his money typifies the nightmare of the Victorian middle class, for whom a man losing his money was like a woman losing her virtue, and in the book Grahame adds significantly, 'all that makes life worth living'. His boyhood had been marred by financial as well as emotional troubles. When his mother died in 1864 (Grahame was five years old at the time), his father made scant provision for the four children, despatching them to live with a grandmother in Cookham Dene. And towards the end of his life, when he discovered how much commission his agent Curtis Brown was taking on foreign translations, Grahame complained with Toad-like intensity:

'My dear C-B . . . When I read your classic periods, so firm yet so tender, I wilted, I sagged, I crumpled. I shed bitter tears. I finally collapsed on the floor, a sodden heap of misery . . .'

could hear the puffing of steam-engines not very far off, & he saw some red & green lights through the trees, & he said to himself "That must be a railway station, & if I am to get home the first thing to do is to get in to a train that goes there". So he made his way down to the station & went into the ticket office & asked for a ticket. And the man said "Where for?" and the toad told him, and the man said "That will cost five shillings". So the toad felt for his pocket, to find his money, when to his honor & dismay he couldn't find any pocket! Because he had got the washerwoman's dress on. Then he remembered that when he had changed clothes in such a hurry he had left all his money, & his keys, & pencil, & matches, & everything, in the pockets of the clothes he had taken off. So there he was, miles & miles from home, dressed like a washerwoman, without a penny of money. Then Mr Toad shed bitter tears, & said to the man "Please I have lost all my money - will you be very kind & give me a ticket for nothing?"

Fowey Hotel, Cornwall
28 May 1907

When Curtis Brown asked him, *à propos* of illustrations, whether Toad was life-size or train-size, Grahame replied that he was both and neither: the Toad was train-size, the train was Toad-size, and therefore illustrations were out of the question.

Eventually, when sales slackened (there were four editions in the first six months and only three over the next four years), Grahame relented, and the first illustrated editions were by Paul Bransom (1913), Nancy Barnhart (1922) and Wyndham Payne (1927). But it is the work of E. H. Shepard (1931) and Arthur Rackham (1940) that has stood the test of time. Before undertaking the task, Shepard visited Grahame, then in his seventies. Grahame said to him: 'I love these little people, be kind to them'.

But this man only laughed, and said "Go away old woman! We don't carry washerwomen for nothing on this railway!" So the toad went away crying, and wandered down the platform by the side of the train, thinking whatever should he do, till he came to where the engine was. And the engine-driver saw he was crying, & said cheerfully "What's the matter, mother?" And the toad replied "I want to get home, so badly, but I've lost all my money & I can't buy a ticket". Now the engine-driver was a kind-hearted man, & he said "Look here, washerwoman! This engine-driving is very dirty work, and I dirty so many shirts that my wife says she's tired of washing 'em. If you will wash two shirts for me, next week, I'll let you ride on the engine with me now, & so you will get home for nothing!" Then the toad was overjoyed, and he sprang up on the engine with great delight. Of course he had never washed a shirt in his life, and couldn't if he tried, but he thought "When I get home, & get some more money, I will send the engine-driver some, to pay for his washing, & that will be just the same". Presently the engine-driver blew his whistle & the train began to move out of the station; & soon they were puffing & rattling through the country, ever so fast, & the toad was jumping up & down with sheer delight, to think that soon he would be home again.

Suddenly the engine-driver began to listen & presently he said It's very funny, but I believe I hear another train following us! The toad began to feel nervous. Then the engine-driver looked over the back of the train, for the moon was shining brightly & he could see a long way down the line, & at last he cried out 'Yes! I can see an engine! It is coming along very fast. I believe we are being pursued!' And the toad began to feel very nervous. Presently the engine-driver looked again & then he cried 'Yes, they are gaining on us! I can see them clearly now! It is an engine pursuing us! It is full of policemen, and they are all brandishing revolvers & calling out 'Stop, Stop, Stop, Stop, STOP!!!!

This is all the news I have up to the present time.
Your affectionate
Daddy

Fowey Hotel, Cornwall
28 May 1907

Escape and pursuit are natural ingredients of a children's story, but the concentrated power of the chase sequences in the letters and later in the book may owe something to Grahame's own situation.

In 1907 a new Governor had been appointed to the Bank of England and Grahame, it seems, was under strong pressure to change his leisurely approach: he took long holidays, and was frequently observed 'striding through the Secretary's outer office shortly before four o'clock'. In June 1908, four months before the book was published, he resigned, officially for reasons of ill-health. If this were really the reason, it is odd that his pension was meagre, and there is no word of sympathy or gratitude in the final communication from the Bank.

Suddenly the engine-driver began to listen; and presently he said - "It's very funny, but I do believe I hear another train following us!" The toad began to feel nervous. Then the engine-driver looked over the back of the train, for the moon was shining brightly & he could see a long way down the line, & at last he cried out "Yes! I see an engine! It is coming along very fast. I believe we are being pursued!" And the toad began to feel very nervous. Presently the engine-driver looked again, & then he cried "Yes, they are gaining on us! I can see them clearly now! It is an engine pursuing us! It is full of policemen, and they are all brandishing revolvers & calling out : Stop, Stop, Stop, Stop

STOP !!!!

This is all the news I have up to the present time

Your affectionate

Daddy

'The little grey sea town' – Fowey Harbour, c.1905.

Fowey Hotel, Cornwall
31 May 1907

In the book, Fowey is immortalized as:

> 'the little grey sea town . . . that clings along one steep side of the harbour.
> There through dark doorways you look down flights of stone steps, overhung
> by great pink tufts of valerian and ending in a patch of sparkling blue
> water . . . the salmon leap on the flood tide, schools of mackerel flash and play
> past quay-sides and foreshores, and by the windows the great vessels glide,
> night and day, up to their moorings or forth to the open sea.'

Grahame had made many imaginary 'sea-trips' and journeys with
Mouse. The sofa would become a train or a boat, and Grahame would be
ordered to get into the 'tofa-boat', row out a long way, let down lines and
wait for a 'wriggle'. On one train-journey 'till tea-ready', Mouse was only
enticed to the table by the 'guard' announcing: 'Ten minutes for
freshmints!'

TELEPHONE 0197.

The FOWEY HOTEL

FOWEY, CORNWALL, 31st May, 1907.

My dearest Mouse

I hope you are quite well.
I am very glad to hear that you have
been having some boating, and sea-trips
to America & other distant lands.
Now you may like to hear something
further about poor toad. When Toad
heard that they were being pursued
by an engine full of policemen with
revolvers, he fell on his knees among
the coals & cried out "O kind Mr.
Engine-driver, save me, save me, & I
will confess everything! I am not

the washerwoman I seem to be! I am a toad – the well-known Mr. Toad, of Toad Hall & I have escaped from prison, & those policemen are coming to recapture me!' Then the engine-driver looked very grave, & said 'What were you in prison for, toad?' And the toad blushed deeply & said 'I only borrowed a motor-car while the people were having lunch. I didn't mean to steal it really.' 'Well', said the engine-driver, 'you have evidently been a bad toad. But I will save you if I can.' So he piled more coals on the fire, & the engine flew over the rails; but the engine behind kept gaining & gaining, & presently the engine-driver said with a sigh 'I'm afraid it's no use. They must catch us up soon, & then they will climb along our train till they get to our engine, & if we attempt to resist they will shoot us dead with their revolvers.' Then the toad said 'O dear kind Mr. Engine-driver, do think of something to save me!' And the engine-driver

Fowey Hotel, Cornwall
31 May 1907

Again the book is less dramatic here. Grahame omits the engine driver's grim warning that 'if we attempt to resist, they will shoot us dead', which fuels Toad's panic.

the washerwoman I seem to be! I am a toad – the well-known Mr Toad, of Toad Hall – & I have escaped from prison, & those policemen are coming to re-capture me!" Then the engine-driver looked very grave, & said – what were you in prison for, toad?" And the toad blushed deeply & said – I only borrowed a motor-car while the people were having lunch. I didn't mean to steal it really."

"Well", said the engine-driver. " you have evidently been a bad toad. But I will save you if I can". So he piled more coals on the fire, & the engine flew over the rails; but the engine behind kept gaining & gaining; & presently the engine-driver said with a sigh "I'm afraid it's no use. They must catch us up soon, & then they will climb along our train till they get to our engine, & if we attempt to resist they will shoot us dead with their revolvers". Then the toad said "O dear kind Mr Engine-driver, do think of something to save me!". And the engine-driver

thought a bit and then he said 'There's just
one thing I can do, & it's your only chance.
We are coming to a long tunnel, & on the
other side of the tunnel is a thick wood.
I will put on all speed while we are
running through the tunnel, & as soon
as we are through I will 'slow up' for
a few seconds, & you must jump off
& run into the wood & hide yourself before
the other engine gets through the tunnel,
& then I will go on at full speed & they
will continue to chase me, thinking
you are still on the train.'
    Next moment they shot into the tunnel,
& the engine-driver piled on more coals, & the
sparks flew, & the train rushed & roared &
rattled through the tunnel, [till] at last they
shot out into the moonlight [at] on the other
side, [end and saw the wood, looking back] & then the engine-driver put on his
brakes hard & the train slowed down to
almost a walking pace & the toad got
down on the step & the engine-driver
said 'Now jump!' and the toad
jumped, & rolled down the embankment
& scrambled into the wood & hid himself.

thought a bit & then he said "There is just one thing I can do, & its your only chance. We are coming to a long tunnel, & on the other side of the tunnel is a thick wood. I will put on all speed while we are running through the tunnel, & as soon as we are through I will "slow up" for a few seconds, & you must jump off & run into the wood & hide yourself before the other engine gets through the tunnel, & then I will go on at full speed & they will continue to chase me, thinking you are still on the train."

Next moment they shot into the tunnel, & the engine-driver piled on more coals, & the sparks flew, & the train rushed & roared & rattled through the tunnel, & at last they shot out into the moonlight on the other side, & then the engine-driver put on his brakes hard & the train slowed down to almost a walking pace & the toad got down on the step & the engine-driver said "Now jump!" and the toad jumped, & rolled down the embankment & scrambled into the wood & hid himself.

Then he peeped out & saw the train get
up speed again & go off very fast. And
presently the other engine came roaring
& whistling out of the tunnel, in hot
pursuit, with the policemen waving
their revolvers & shouting 'Stop, Stop,
Stop!!! Then the toad had a good
laugh – for the first time since he was
put into prison.

But it was now very late, & dark, & cold,
& here he was in a wild wood, with no money
& no friends. And little animals peeped out
of their holes & pointed at him & made fun
of him; & a fox came slinking by, & said
'Hullo washerwoman! how's the washing
business doing?' and sniggered. And the
toad looked for a stone to throw at him,
& couldn't find one, which made him sad.
Presently he came to a hollow tree, full
of dry leaves; & there he curled himself
up as comfortably as he could, & slept till
the morning.

In my next letter I will try to tell
you the Adventure of the Toad & the Bargee;
and about the Gipsy, & how the Toad went
into Horse-dealing.
Ever your affectionate
Daddy.

Fowey Hotel, Cornwall
31 May 1907

In the book, the wood is not 'wild' but 'unknown', and 'the Wild Wood',
always in capitals, is the dark, sinister hunting-ground of the weasels,
ferrets and stoats: the notorious Wild Wooders.

The next four letters cover the events described in Chapter 10: 'The
Further Adventures of Toad'.

Then he peeped out & saw the train get up speed again & go off very fast. And presently the other engine came roaring & whistling out of the tunnel, in hot pursuit, with the policemen waving their revolvers & shouting "Stop. Stop. Stop!!!" Then the toad had a good laugh — for the first time since he was put into prison.

But it was now very late, & dark, & cold, & here he was in a wild wood, with no money & no friends. And little animals peeped out of their holes & pointed at him & made fun of him; & a fox came slinking by, & said "Hullo washerwoman! how's the washing business doing?" and sniggered. And the toad looked for a stone to throw at him, & couldn't find one, which made him sad. Presently he came to a hollow tree, full of dry leaves; & there he curled himself up as comfortably as he could, & slept till the morning.

In my next letter I will try to tell you the Adventure of the Toad & the Bargee; & about the Gipsy, & how the Toad went into Horse-dealing.

Ever your affectionate
Daddy

Fowey Hotel, Cornwall
7 June 1907

'Boats are the only things worth living for – any sort', wrote Grahame. As
a schoolboy he 'glided through the hayfields' of Oxfordshire in a canoe; as
a young man he sculled on the Thames in London, and in Cornwall he
discovered the excitement of deep-sea fishing. His honeymoon was largely
spent sailing and rowing, and he was a life-long member of the Royal
Fowey Yacht Club.

In *The Wind in the Willows*, the Water Rat explains the addiction:

> 'Nice? It's the *only* thing . . . there is *nothing* – absolutely nothing – half so
> much worth doing as simply messing about in boats . . . In or out of 'em, it
> doesn't matter. Nothing seems really to matter, that's the charm of it.
> Whether you get away or whether you don't; whether you arrive at your
> destination or whether you reach somewhere else, or whether you never get
> anywhere at all, you're always busy, and you never do anything in
> particular; and when you've done it there's always something else to do, and
> you can do it if you like, but you'd much better not.'

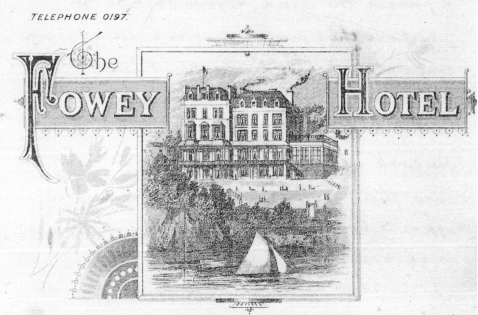

TELEPHONE 0197.

The FOWEY HOTEL

FOWEY, CORNWALL, 7th June 1907.

My dearest Mouse

I hope you are having better
weather than we are getting here. It is so wet
& windy here that we cannot go out rowing in
boats, or fly kites, or sail, or anything.

You may be wishing to hear what
further things happened to Toad on his way
home, after his escape from the policemen who
were pursuing him to take him back to prison.
Well, next morning the sun shone brightly into
the hollow tree, & woke up Mr. Toad, who was
sleeping soundly after his fatiguing exertions
of the previous day. He got up, shook himself,
combed the dead leaves out of his hair with
his fingers; & set off walking briskly, for he was

Fowey Hotel, Cornwall
7 June 1907

In the book, the bargee becomes the barge-woman, and the incident is
enriched because Toad's downfall is caused by his own ludicrous boasting.
When asked if he is '*very* fond of washing', he replies:

> 'I love it ... I simply dote on it. Never so happy as when I've got both arms in
> the wash-tub ... A real pleasure, I assure you, ma'am!'

When the barge-woman calls his bluff, his misery at the wash-tub is
total:

> 'His back ached badly, and he noticed with dismay that his paws were
> beginning to get all crinkly ... He muttered under his breath words that
> should never pass the lips of either washerwomen or Toads; and lost the
> soap, for the fiftieth time.'

very cold & rather hungry. Well, he walked & he walked,
till he came to a canal, & he thought that must lead
to a town, so he walked along the tow-path, &
presently he met a horse, with a long rope attached
to it, towing a barge; & he waited for the barge
to come up, & there was a man steering it, & he
nodded, & said 'Goodmorning, washerwoman!
what are you doing here?' Then the toad made
a pitifull face, & said "Please, kind Sir, I am
going to pay a visit to my married daughter,
who lives near a fine house called 'Toad Hall';
but I've lost my way, & spent all my money, &
I'm very tired". Then the man said "Toad Hall?
why, I'm going that way myself. Jump in,
& I'll give you a lift." So he steered the barge
close to the bank, & the toad stepped on
board & sat down, very pleased with himself.
Presently the man said "I don't see why I should
give you a lift for nothing, so you take that
tub of water standing over there, & that bit of
yellow soap, & here are some shirts, & you can
be washing them as we go along". Then the toad
was rather frightened, for he had never washed
a shirt in his life; but he dabbed the shirt into
the water, & he dabbed some soap on it, but
it never seemed to get any cleaner, & his
fingers got very cold & he began to get
very cross. Presently the man came to
see how he was getting on, & burst out
laughing at him, & said "Call yourself a
washerwoman? That's not the way to wash

Fowey Hotel, Cornwall
7 June 1907

Toad is both animal and human, as this incident shows. He is Mr Toad of
Toad Hall, and 'nothing but an old toad', who can be picked up by a
hindleg and thrown overboard.

a shirt, you very silly old woman!" Then the toad lost his temper, & quite forgot himself, & said "Don't you dare to speak to your betters like that! And don't call me a silly old woman! I'm no more an old woman than you are yourself, you common, low, vulgar bargee!" Then the bargee looked closely at him, & cried out "Why, no, I can see you're not really a washerwoman at all! You're nothing but an old toad!" Then he grabbed the toad by one hind-leg & one fore-leg, & swung him round & sent him flying through the air .... Like that — Splosh!! He found himself head-over-ears in the water!

When the toad came to the surface he wiped the water out of his eyes & struck out for the shore; but the woman's dress he was wearing got round his legs, & made it very hard work. When at last he was safely on the tow-path again, he saw the barge disappearing in the distance, & the man looking back & laughing at him. This made Mr. Toad mad with rage. He tucked the wet skirt up well under his arms, & ran as hard as he could along the path,

Fowey Hotel, Cornwall
7 June 1907

Miss Stott later wrote that Mouse 'loved that motor-boat trip' to the Black
Rabbit Inn near Arundel, 'saying little but getting impressions'.

& passed the barge, & ran on till he overtook the horse that was towing it, and unfastened the tow-rope, & jumped on the horse's back, & dug his heels into its sides, & off they went at a gallop! He took one look back as they went, & he saw that the barge had run into the opposite bank of the canal, & stuck, & the bargee was shaking his fist at him & calling out 'Stop, stop, stop!! But the toad never stopped, but only laughed & galloped on & on & on, across country, over fields & hedges, until he had left the canal, & the barge, & the bargee, miles & miles behind him

I am afraid the Gipsy will have to wait till the next letter.

Your affectionate

Daddy

I am so glad to hear you have been out in a motor boat

'The gipsy took his pipe out.' An Arthur Rackham
illustration for *The Wind in the Willows* (1940).

16 Durham Villas, London
21 June 1907

The holiday over, Grahame was now back in London. The remaining ten
letters were written in 16 Durham Villas, which had been the Grahames'
home for the first six years of their marriage and, following their move to
Cookham Dene in 1906, was retained as a *pied-à-terre*.

In London 'he looked all *wrong*', wrote his friend, Graham Robertson:

> 'As he strode along the pavements one felt to him as towards a huge St.
> Bernard or Newfoundland dog, a longing to take him away into the open
> country where he could be let off the lead and allowed to range at will. He
> appeared happy enough and made the best of everything, as do the dogs, but
> he was too big for London and it hardly seemed kind of Fate to keep him
> there.'

Grahame was also like an animal in his sensitivity to smells. In the
book, the smell of the cooking 'seemed like the very soul of Nature taking
form and appearing to her children, a true Goddess, a mother of solace and
comfort.' He loved the 'foreign smells' of France and Italy, and once wrote:
'A change of smells is as cheering as a change of air, cooking and custom.'

16, Durham Villas, Campden Hill. W.

21 June 1907.

My dearest Mouse

No doubt you will be interested to hear the further adventures of Mr Toad, after he gallopped away across country on the bargee's horse, with the bargee shouting after him in vain. Well presently the horse got tired of galloping so fast, and broke from a gallop into a trot, and then from a trot into a walk, & then he stopped altogether & began to nibble grass. And the toad looked round about him & found he was on a large common. On the common stood a gipsy tent, and a gipsy man was sitting beside it, on a bucket turned upside-down, smoking. In front of the tent a fire of sticks was burning, & over the fire hung an iron pot, and out of the pot came steam, & bubblings, and the most beautiful good smell that ever you smelt.

Then the toad felt very hungry indeed, for he had
had no breakfast that morning, & no supper the
night before; so he sniffed & sniffed, & looked
at the pot, & the gipsy; & the gipsy sat &
smoked, & looked back at him.

Presently the gipsy took his pipe out of his
mouth & said 'Like to sell that there horse
of yours?' (Now you must understand
that gipsies are very fond of buying &
selling horses, & never miss an opportunity.)

This was an entirely new idea to Toad.
He had never thought of trying to sell the
horse; but now he saw a way of getting
a little money, which he wanted so badly.
So he said, 'What, sell this beautiful
young animal o' mine? No, I can't say
I had thought of selling this beautiful
young animal o' mine. You see it's such a
beautiful young animal – half an Arab
& half a Race-Horse & half a Prize Hackney.
However, how much might you feel disposed

Then the Toad felt very hungry indeed, for he had had no breakfast that morning, & no supper the night before; so he sniffed & sniffed. & looked at the pot, & the gipsy; & the gipsy sat & smoked, & looked back at him.

Presently the gipsy took his pipe out of his mouth & said "Like to sell that there horse of yours?" (Now you must understand that gipsies are very fond of buying & selling horses, & never miss an opportunity)

This was an entirely new idea to Toad. He had never thought of trying to sell the horse; but now he saw a way of getting a little money, which he wanted so badly. So he said, "What. sell this beautiful young animal o'mine? No, I can't say I had thought of selling this beautiful young animal o'mine. You see its such a beautiful young animal – half an Arab & half a Race Horse & half a Prize Hackney However, how much might you feel disposed

to give me for this very beautiful young animal
o' mine?'

The gipsy looked at the horse, & he looked at
the Toad, & he looked at the horse again, & then
he said 'Shillin' a leg', & turned away &
went on smoking.

'A shilling a leg'? said Mr. Toad – 'please
I shall want a little time to work that out,
& add it up, & see what it comes to.' So
he climbed down off the horse & left it to
graze, & sat down by the gipsy, & counted
on his fingers, & did sums in his head, &
presently he said 'A shilling a leg? Why, that
comes to exactly four shillings. O no. I could
not think of selling this beautiful young
animal for four shillings.'

'Well', said the gipsy, 'I'll tell you what I'll
do. I'll make it five shillings & that's a shilling
more than he's worth; and that's my last word.'

Then the toad pondered deeply. For he
was penniless, & five shillings seemed a very
large sum of money. On the other hand, it

16 Durham Villas, London
21 June 1907

Grahame was fascinated by the wandering life. He loved circuses and in
one of his earliest essays, 'A Bohemian in Exile', told of a modern scholar-
gypsy who broke loose and contracted out of society. Again 'Long Odds',
published in *The Yellow Book*, is a story about an expatriate Englishman
who, 'with the mark of Cheapside still evident on him . . . worked South till
he came to Venice', and Grahame too, like Rat, was sorely tempted to go
'South . . . to the shores that are calling me'. But the call of the Bank and
respectability always prevailed and he went south only for holidays.

to give me for this very beautiful young animal o' mine?"

The gipsy looked at the horse, & he looked at the Toad, & he looked at the horse again, & then he said "Shillin' a leg", & turned away & went on smoking.

"A shilling a leg"? said Mr Toad - "please I shall want a little time to work that out, & add it up, & see what it comes to." So he climbed down off the horse & left it to graze, & sat down by the gipsy, & counted on his fingers, & did sums in his head, & presently he said "a shilling a leg" Why, that comes to exactly four shillings. O no. I could not think of selling this beautiful young animal for four shillings."

"Well", said the gipsy, "I'll tell you what I'll do. I'll make it five shillings & that's a shilling more than he's worth; & that's my last word."

Then the toad pondered deeply. For he was penniless, & five shillings seemed a very large sum of money. On the other hand, it

did not seem very much to get for a horse. But
then the horse hadn't cost him anything, so
it was all clear profit. At last he said, 'Look
here, gipsy. You shall give me six shillings
& sixpence, cash, & as-much breakfast as
I can eat, out of that iron pot of yours
that keeps sending forth such delicious
smells. And I will give you my fine young
horse & all the beautiful harness that is
on him.' Well the gipsy grumbled a bit,
but at last he agreed. And he counted out
six shillings & sixpence into toad's paw; &
then he fetched plates out of the tent, &
poured hot stew into them out of the
pot; & it was the most beautiful stew,
made of partridges & pheasants & chickens
& hares & rabbits & pea-hens & guinea fowls.
And the toad stuffed & stuffed, & kept
asking for more, & thought that he had
never eaten so good a breakfast in all his
life.
Your affectionate
    Daddy

did not seem very much to get for a horse. But then the horse hadn't cost him anything, so it was all clear profit. At last he said, "Look here, gipsy. You shall give me six shillings & sixpence, cash, & as much breakfast as I can eat, out of that iron pot of yours that keeps sending forth such delicious smells. And I will give you my fine young horse & all the beautiful harness that is on him." Well the gipsy grumbled a bit, but at last he agreed. And he counted out six shillings & sixpence into toad's paw; & then he fetched plates out of the tent; & poured hot stew into them out of the pot; & it was the most beautiful stew, made of partridges & pheasants & chickens & hares & rabbits & pea-hens & guinea fowl. And the toad stuffed & stuffed, & kept asking for more, & thought that he had never eaten so good a breakfast in all his life.

Your affectionate
Daddy

16 Durham Villas, London
17 July 1907

Nearly a month has elapsed since the last letter, and yet Grahame begins at the exact point where he left off – presumably he was now making careful notes. As the story gathers detail and momentum and becomes a full-scale narrative, the relationship between father and son seems gradually to cool. There is no longer even the perfunctory interest in Mouse's news from Littlehampton, nor apparently are the letters addressed to him. This followed Mouse's announcement that he was changing his name to Michael Robinson – a far finer name, he claimed, than Alastair Grahame. From now on there are no preambles and each letter ends simply 'to be continued'. There are no words of affection, since Grahame maintained that he was incapable of familiarity towards a complete stranger.

16, Durham Villas, Campden Hill. W.

17 July, 1907

My dear Robinson

WELL!

So when the Toad had stuffed
as much breakfast inside of him as
he could possibly hold, he stood up,
and shook hands with the Gipsy and
said goodbye to him, + said goodbye
to the horse, + set off in the direction
of Toad Hall. And by this time he was
feeling very happy, for the sun was shining
brightly, + his wet clothes were quite
dry again, + he had had a first-rate
breakfast, + he had got money in his
pocket, + he was getting near his home.
And he thought of his adventures, +
all the dangers he had escaped, + he
began to be very proud + stuck-up, and
"Ho ho," he said to himself as he
tramped along, "What a clever animal

I am! There is no one like me in the whole
world! My enemies shut me up in prison;
I escape [by sheer ability & daring] with the greatest ease. They pursue
me with engines & policemen & revolvers;
I simply laugh at [the whole crowd of] them & disappear.
I am [unfortunately] thrown into canals; [what of it?] I swim to land,
seize a horse, [escape on horse] sell it for a pocketful of
money, get breakfasts given me & am made
welcome wherever I go! Ho ho! I am The
Toad, the handsome, the popular, the glorious
Toad!' Then he got so puffed up with pride
& conceit that he made up a song, in praise
of himself, & sang it as he walked along.
O it was a conceited song! Here are some
of the verses:—

    The world has held great Heroes,
    As history-books have showed,
    But [never a name, to go down to fame] none so divine, or half so fine
    As the famous Mr. [Compared with that of] Toad!

16 Durham Villas, London
17 July 1907

As a schoolboy, Grahame had dreamed of becoming one of Oxford's 'clever
men', but was denied the opportunity by an uncle who, despite Grahame's
pleas, insisted on his entering the Bank of England. All his life he felt 'the
spell of Oxford' with 'the good grey Gothic on the one hand, and, on the
other, the cool secluded reaches of the Thames – the "stripling Thames",
remote and dragon-fly haunted.' Almost the last thing Grahame wrote
was to be the nostalgic essay, 'Oxford through a Boy's Eyes'.

I am! There is no one like me in the whole world! My enemies shut me up in prison; I escape with the greatest ease. They pursue me with engines & policemen & revolvers; I simply laugh at them & disappear. I am thrown into canals; I swim to land, seize a horse, sell it for a pocketful of money, get breakfasts given me & am made welcome wherever I go! Ho ho! I am The Toad, the handsome, the popular, the glorious Toad!" Then he got so puffed up with pride & conceit that he made up a song, in praise of himself, & sang it as he walked along. O it _was_ a conceited song! Here are some of the verses:—

The world has held great Heroes,
As history-books have showed,
But never a name to go down to fame
compared with that of
As the famous Mr. Toad!

The clever men at Oxford
Know all that there is to be knowed;
But they none of them know one half as
                                    much
As intelligent Mr. Toad!

16 Durham Villas, London
17 July 1907

As a young man, Grahame had joined the Volunteers and became a drill
sergeant. He paraded with his regiment, the London Scottish, on Queen
Victoria's Jubilee Day: 'a great day', he wrote, 'full of music, marching
and much true and affectionate loyalty and patriotism.'

The explicit moralizing here, which is omitted in the book, is a
reminder that the story is still partly a cautionary tale for a Toad-like son.

14

The animals sat in the Ark & cried,
Their tears in torrents flowed;
Who was it said "There's land ahead"?
Encouraging Mr. Toad!

The Army all saluted
As they marched along the road.
— Was it the King? — or Kitchener?
No; it was Mr. Toad.

The Queen and her Ladies-in-waiting
Sat at the window and sewed.
She cried "Look! who's that handsome
                                    man?"
They answered: "Mr. Toad!"

This was the sort of stuff that he sang,
the conceited animal. But his pride
was soon to have a fall. Let it be a
lesson to us, not to be so puffed up
& conceited as the proud Toad.

Presently he came to the high-road
which ran past the common; and as
he glanced up it, he saw, very far away,
a dark speck, which gradually grew

16 Durham Villas, London
17 July 1907

The diminutive 'Dy' (short for Daddy) is the last mention of father or son in the sequence.

larger & larger & larger ; & then he heard
a faint humming noise, which gradually
grew louder & louder & louder ; & then
he heard a very well known sound, & that
was

Poop ! poop !

"Ho ho!" said the Toad," this is life, this
is what I like ! I will stop them & ask
them to give me a lift, & so I will drive
up to Toad Hall in triumph on a motor-
car ! And perhaps I shall be able to
— borrow that motor-car." He did not
say "steal", but I fear the wicked animal
thought it. He stepped out into the road
to hail the car, when suddenly his face
turned very pale, his knees trembled &
shook, & he had a bad pain in his tummy.
Why was this ? Because he had suddenly
recognized the car as the very one he
had stolen out of the yard of the
Red Lion Hotel ! And the people sitting
inside were the very people who had gone
into the Hotel for refreshments on that
fatal day! (To be continued)

16 Durham Villas, London
7 August 1907

Grahame seems to be enjoying the new-found anonymity; it frees him to concentrate entirely on the story. Yet Mouse's wish to change his name may have been more significant than his father realized. The boy's letters from Littlehampton, where he also spent the next three summers, and from Cookham Dene, contain resentment at his parents' frequent absences. He missed them, appealing to them individually and together – 'Dear Mum and Co' – to come and see him:

'Could you come down here for the week end please do!'

And when the appeals were in vain:

'Dear Dad, I hope you and Mum have got my last letter, Thine Bad Boy.'

15

16, Durham Villas, Campden Hill. W.

7th August, 1907.

My dear Michael Robinson

When the Toad saw that his enemies
were close upon him, his heart turned to water,
his muscles failed, & he sank down in a
shabby miserable heap in the road, murmuring
to himself "It's all up! It's all over now!
Prison again! Dry bread & water again!
Chains & policemen again! O what a fool
I have been! What did I want to go
strutting about the country for, singing
conceited songs, instead of going quietly
home by back ways & hiding, until it
all blew over! O unhappy toad! O
miserable animal!" and his head
sank down in the dust.

The terrible motor car drew nearer
& nearer & nearer. Then it stopped.
Some gentlemen got out. They walked
round the trembling heap of misery lying

in the road, & one of them said – "O dear! Here is a poor old washerwoman who has fainted in the road! Perhaps she is overcome by the heat, poor thing, or perhaps she has not had enough food! Anyhow, let us lift her into the motor-car & take her to the nearest village."

So they tenderly lifted the toad into the motor-car & propped him up on the cushions, & started off. When the toad heard them talk in that kind way, & knew that he was not recognized, his courage began to revive, & he opened one of his eyes. Then one of the gentlemen said: "See, she is better already! The fresh air is doing her good! How do you feel now, washerwoman?"

The toad answered in a feeble voice – "Thank you kindly, Sir, I'm feeling rather better. I think if I might sit on the front seat, beside the chauffeur, where I could get more air, I should soon be quite right again".

"That's a very sensible woman" said the gentleman. So they helped her him into the front seat, beside the chauffeur, & on

went the car. The toad began to sit up, & look
about him, & presently he said to the chauffeur
" Please Mr. chauffeur, I wish you would
let me try to drive the car for a little ;
it looks so easy ; I'm sure I could do
it quite well ! "

The chauffeur laughed, heartily. But
one of the gentlemen said " Bravo, washerwoman !
I like your spirit ! Let her try. She won't
do any harm."

So the chauffeur gave up his seat to the
toad, & he took the steering wheel in his hands,
& set the car going, & off they went, very slowly
& carefully at first, for the toad was prudent.
The gentlemen clapped their hands, & cried
" Bravo, washerwoman ! How well she
does it ! Fancy a washerwoman driving
a motor car ! Bravo !

Then the Toad went a little faster.
The gentlemen applauded. The Toad went
faster still.

Then, when when he felt the air
singing past his ears, & the car throbbing

16 Durham Villas, London
7 August 1907

This is the longest letter yet and the closest so far to the book.
Increasingly, as the character matures in Grahame's mind, 'the toad' is
becoming 'the Toad'. By the end of the letter-sequence, he is most often
simply 'Toad'.

under him, the Toad began to lose his head. He went faster & faster still. The gentlemen called out warningly "Be careful, washerwoman!" Then the Toad lost his head entirely. He stood up in his seat & shouted "Ho ho! who are you calling washerwoman! I am the Toad! the famous Mr Toad! The motor-car-driver, the toad who always escapes, who baffles his enemies, who dodges policemen, who breaks out of prison, the always-victorious, the triumphant Toad!"

Then the gentlemen & the chauffeur arose & flung themselves upon him. "Seize him!" they cried. "Seize the toad, the wicked animal who stole our motor-car! Bind him, chain him, drag him to the police-station! Down with the Toad!"

Alas! They ought to have remembered to stop the motor-car before playing any pranks of that sort. With a half-turn of the wheel the Toad sent the car crashing through the hedge. Then it gave an enormous bound, and sploosh! it landed in a horse-pond!

16 Durham Villas, London
7 August 1907

In the book, the phrase 'pumped out' is replaced by the less colloquial but also less vivid 'breathless and weary'.

16, Durham Villas, Campden Hill. W.

The Toad found himself flying through the air like a swallow. He was just beginning to wonder whether he would ever come down again or whether he had somehow got a pair of wings & turned into a toad-bird, when bump! He landed on his back. He jumped up at once, & found himself in a meadow. Looking back, he saw the car, almost entirely covered by the water, while the gentlemen & the chauffeur were floundering about in their long thick motor-coats in the pond. He did not stay to help them. No! He set off running at once, & ran & ran & ran, across country, till he was quite pumped out. Then he settled down into a walk, & as he walked along presently he began to giggle, & from

giggling he took to laughing, + he laughed + laughed until he had to sit down under a hedge. "Ho ho!" he roared "The Toad again! Always Mr. Toad! Who got them to give him a lift? Who wanted to sit on the front seat to get fresh air? Who got the chauffeur to let him drive? Who upset them all into the horse-pond? Who escaped, free + unhurt, while they were floundering about in the water? Toad, clever Toad, great Toad, good Toad!" Then he burst into song again, + sang

"The motor-car went poop-poop-poop
As it whizzed along the road;
Who was it steered it into the pond?
Ingenious Mr. Toad!

O how clever I am! How clever, how clever, how clev ——————"

He heard a slight noise behind him. He looked back. O horror! O misery!

16 Durham Villas, London
7 August 1907

Mouse may have had such a scene in mind when he wrote, a few years later in a schoolboy poem:

> Ye fat red-faced policemen
> Ye suffragette pursue,
> Ye magistrate says 'fourteen days'
> Ye suffragette says 'Booh!'

18

O despair! O my!

About two fields behind him, a chauffeur and two large policemen were running towards him as hard as they could!

The toad sprang to his feet & set off running again, his heart in his mouth. " O my!" he gasped as he panted along, " what an ass I am! what a conceited ass? O my! O my! O my! "

He looked back & saw they were gaining on him. He kept looking back as he ran, & saw that they still gained. He struggled on, but he was a fat animal, & his legs were short, & as he looked back he saw that they still gained. They were near him now! He never looked where he was going, but ran on wildly, looking over his shoulder at the approaching enemy, when suddenly

Sploosh!

The toad found himself head over ears in deep water, in a rapid stream. He had run straight into the river!

He rose to the surface, & tried to grasp the reeds & the rushes that grew along the bank, but the stream was so fast that it tore them out of his hands. "O my!" said the poor toad, - "If ever I steal a motor-car again ——" Then down he went, & came up spluttering. Presently he saw a big dark hole in the bank, above his head, & as the stream bore him past he reached out a paw & caught hold of the edge. Then he slowly drew himself up out of the water, till he was able to rest his elbows on the edge of the hole. There he remained for some minutes, puffing & panting, for he was quite exhausted.

Presently, as he gazed into the big dark hole, he saw a tiny speck of light, that looked like a glow-worm, or a distant star. As he looked, it winked & glittered, & got more & more like a tiny eye! He looked & looked, & saw the outline of a tiny face round it!

A dark little face ——
and Whiskers! ——

It   was   the   water-rat!

(To be continued)

'A little village called Golant', c.1905.

16 Durham Villas, London
12 August 1907

Like the other animals in the story, the Water Rat is a complex creation
derived from many sources, not least from Grahame himself. Apart from
his friend Arthur Quiller-Couch, the author and don, Rat owes most
perhaps to another Fowey resident, Edward Atkinson. 'Atky', an elderly
bachelor, had a charming riverside house and shared Grahame's
enthusiasm for journeys to southern Europe and boating expeditions
around Fowey. A trip up river with him 'to a little village called
Golant . . . for tea' in the summer of 1907 is said to have inspired the river
picnic in the first chapter of the book.

The next four letters, written in the space of a fortnight, cover the
events described in Chapter 11: 'Like Summer Tempests Came his Tears',
and at the beginning of Chapter 12: 'The Return of Ulysses'.

19

16, Durham Villas, Campden Hill. W.

12th August, 1907.

Dear Robinson

The Water-Rat put out a neat little brown paw, + gave Toady a big hoist + a pull, over the edge of the hole, + there was Mr. Toad at last, standing safe + sound in the hall, covered with mud, + with the water streaming off him, but pleased + happy at being in a friend's house at last after so many perilous adventures. "O Ratty!" he cried, "I've been having such times, you can't think! Such dangers, such escapes, and all through my own cleverness! Been in prison — got out of it! Been thrown into a canal — swam ashore! Stole a horse — sold him for a pocketful of money! O I am a

smart Toad & no mistake! Tell you
what I did, only just now _____'
   'Toad': – said the Water-Rat firmly:
'You go off up-stairs at once, & take
off that old cotton rag that looks as if
it had once belonged to a washerwoman,
& clean yourself, & put on some of my
clothes & try & look like a gentleman
if you <u>can</u>; for a more shabby be-draggled
disreputable-looking object than you
are I never saw in my life! Now
stop swaggering & be off!' [I'll talk to you later.]

16 Durham Villas, London
12 August 1907

To 'look like a gentleman' was of great importance to the Edwardian
male. Once, in Kensington Gardens, as Mouse and Miss Stott watched
'some street Arabs doing gymnastics on some railings', Mouse remarked
perversely: 'I wish I was like that – not a gentleman!'

smart Toad + no mistake! Tell you what I did, only just now ——————— "

     "Toad": — said the Water-Rat firmly: "You go off up-stairs at once, + take off that old cotton rag that looks as if it had once belonged to a washerwoman, + clean yourself, + put on some of my clothes + try + look like a gentleman if you can; for a more shabby be-draggled disreputable-looking object than you are I never saw in my life! Now stop swaggering + be off!"

     So the Toad went very humbly upstairs to the rat's dressing-room, + changed his clothes, + brushed his hair, + by the time he came down again dinner was ready, + very glad the Toad was to see it, for he was very hungry again by this time, in spite of his good breakfast. There was roast veal, stuffed, + vegetable marrow, + a cherry tart.

16 Durham Villas, London
12 August 1907

In the book, Grahame develops Toad's passion for motor-cars into a manic obsession:

'as if in a dream, all sense of right and wrong, all fear of obvious consequences, seemed temporarily suspended. He increased his pace, and as the car devoured the street and leapt forth on the high road through the open country, he was only conscious that he was Toad once more, Toad at his best and highest, Toad the terror, the traffic-queller, the Lord of the lone trail, before whom all must give way or be smitten into nothingness and everlasting night. He chanted as he flew, and the car responded with sonorous drone; the miles were eaten up under him as he sped he knew not whither, fulfilling his instincts, living his hour, reckless of what might come to him.'

20

While they ate their Dinner the Toad
told the Rat all his adventures, not
forgetting all his own cleverness, &
presence of mind, & cunning; but the
Rat looked very grave. When the Toad
had done, the Rat said "Now Toady,
seriously, don't you see what an old
ass you are? You've been beaten, kicked,
imprisoned, chased, thrown into water;
there's no fun in that. And all because
you tried to steal a motor-car. There's
no need for you to steal motor cars;
you've got lots of money; you can buy
a beauty if you like. When are you going
to be sensible, & a credit to your friends?"

Now the Toad was really a very
good-hearted animal, & never minded
being jawed; so although, while the rat
was talking, he kept saying to himself
"But it was fun, though!" & making
strange suppressed noises inside him,
k.i.i.ck, & poop.p.p. & other sounds
like snorts, or the opening of soda-water
bottles, yet when the rat had done,

16 Durham Villas, London
12 August 1907

As a young man Grahame had smoked a pipe, and was the proud owner of 'a long churchwarden clay pipe with red sealing-wax on the stem'. In an early essay he praised tobacco as 'the true Herb of Grace, and a joy and healing balm'.

he said very nicely & humbly " Quite
right, Ratty! I have been a conceited
old ass, I can see; but I'm going
to be a good Toad, & not do it any
more. As soon as we've had our coffee,
and a smoke, I'm going to stroll down
to Toad Hall, & I'm going to lead a
respectable life there, & have a bit of
dinner for my friends when they come to see
me, & have a pony-chaise to jog about
the country in, just as I used to in the
old days."

"Stroll down to Toad Hall?" cried the
Rat. "What are you talking about?
Haven't you _heard_?"

"Heard what?" said the Toad, turning
rather pale. "Go on, Ratty! what
haven't I heard?"

" Do you mean to tell me " said
the Rat, thumping with his little
fist upon the table, " that you
haven't heard ——————— "

(To be cont?)

Dear Robinson,
  'Do you mean to tell me' shouted
the Water-Rat, thumping with his little
fist upon the table, 'That you've never
heard about the animals?' [Stoats & weasels?]

16 Durham Villas, London
16 August 1907

As the pencilled addition shows, 'the animals' are the stoats and weasels: the Wild Wooders. In the book, Grahame clarifies this point and uses the term generically, to include the river-bankers. 'The animals' ceases in the book, to be pejorative, but carries connotations of status and responsibility. Thus before Toad says, 'I can bear it', Grahame inserts: 'I am an animal again', implying that, whereas humans give way to their emotions, animals are stoic. All his life he had a special respect and affection for them. One visitor to Cookham recalled that, when Grahame showed her the home of a water rat, he said: 'He's quite a friend of mine. Evidently he's gone on some excursion – I shall hear about it one day.'

21

16, Durham Villas, Campden Hill. W.

16th August, 1907.

Dear Robinson,

"Do you mean to tell me" shouted the Water-Rat, thumping with his little fist upon the table, "that you've never heard about the animals?" ~~Stuff and nonsense~~

"n-n-no" murmured the Toad, trembling in every limb.

"— and how they've been & taken Toad Hall?" went on the Rat.

Toad leaned his elbows on the table, & his chin on his hands; & a large tear welled up in each of his eyes, overflowed, & splashed on the table, plop! plop!

"Go on, Ratty" he murmured: "tell me all; I can bear it".

"When you - got into that trouble of yours" said the Rat, slowly and impressively: I mean when you - disappeared, you know, over that you-know-what _____'

The Toad nodded.

'Well, it was a good deal talked about
here, naturally,' said the Rat. 'Not only
in the village, [along the riverside] but [even] in the wild-wood. And
the animals went about saying that this
time you would never come back, never,
never!' ['You were done for this time.']

The Toad nodded.
[That's the sort of little beasts they are]
'_____ But the Mole and the Badger' continued
the Water-Rat 'They held out that you
would come back somehow; they didn't
know how, but somehow.'

16 Durham Villas, London
16 August 1907

The 'you-know-what' is of course the motor-car that Toad stole from the
Red Lion Hotel in the first letter.

you - know - what ———"

The Toad nodded.

"Well, it was a good deal talked about here, naturally," said the Rat. "Not only in the village, but in the wild - wood. And the animals went about saying that this time you would never come back, never, never!"

The Toad nodded.

"——— But the Mole & the Badger" continued the Water Rat "They held out that you would come back somehow; they didn't know how, but somehow."

The Toad sat up in his chair, & began to smirk a little.

"——— So the Mole & the Badger" went on the Rat "determined they would move their things in to Toad Hall, & sleep there, to look after it for you. The fact is, they didn't trust the animals!"

"I should think not indeed!" said Toad.

"One dark night" said the Rat, lowering his voice, "One very dark night ——— and

In February 1886 a meeting held in Trafalgar Square to call attention to unemployment turned into a riot. Shops were looted in Piccadilly, the windows of gentlemen's clubs were smashed in Pall Mall, and for two hours the mob was in control. There were no casualties, but London – and Grahame – had glimpsed revolution.

it was blowing hard too, & raining cats-&-
dogs — a band of weasels, armed to the
teeth, crept silently up the carriage-drive.
At the same time a band of desperate
ferrets advanced through the kitchen-garden;
& a number of stoats who stuck at nothing
surrounded the back-door.

The mole & the badger were sitting by the
fire, smoking & telling each other stories, when
these bloodthirsty villains broke down the doors
& rushed in upon them. They made the best
fight they could, but what are two people
against hundreds? They took & beat them
severely, with sticks, the two poor faithful
creatures, & turned them out into the cold &
the wet!

Here the Toad sniggered a little, & then
pulled himself up & tried to look very solemn.

" — And they've been living in Toad Hall ever since"
continued the Rat, "and going on anyhow!
Lying in bed half the day, & breakfast at all
hours, & the place in such a mess its not fit
to be seen! Eating your grub, & drinking
your drink, & making jokes about you,

16 Durham Villas, London
16 August 1907

In November 1903 a respectably dressed man entered Grahame's office, thrust a document at him, and ordered him to read it. When Grahame refused, the man produced a large service revolver and fired twice. Escaping unhurt into the corridor, Grahame summoned help, and 'after some trouble' the man was taken to Cloak Lane police station, where he was charged with 'Wandering in Threadneedle Street: deemed to be a lunatic'. It transpired that he held 'Socialistic views', and was sent to Broadmoor.

Grahame received many letters of sympathy and congratulation, and *Punch* observed that he must be wondering about the expression, 'As safe as the Bank of England'.

& singing vulgar songs about you & about
– prisons & magistrates & all that: & they
tell everybody they've come to stay for good!

"O have they?" said Toad, getting up
& seizing his stick. "I'll jolly soon see
about that!"

"It's no good, Toad!" called the Rat
after him. "You'd better come back!
You'll only get into trouble!"

But the Toad was off, & there was
no holding him. He marched valiantly
down the road, his stick over his shoulder,
till he got near the front gate, when
suddenly behind the palings there popped
up a long yellow ferret with a gun.

"Who comes there?" cried the ferret.

"Stuff & nonsense" said the Toad
angrily. – What do you mean by talking
like that to me? What do you ———"

The ferret said never a word, but
he brought his gun up to his shoulder.
The Toad dropped flat in the road.
Bang! a bullet whistled over his head.

16 Durham Villas, London
16 August 1907

Toad Hall probably contains elements of several houses by the River Thames, 'but I have always felt sure that Toad Hall was on the Oxfordshire side', wrote Grahame to a lady from Whitchurch. This, combined with E. H. Shepard's drawing, suggests that Mapledurham House (across the river from Purley in Berkshire) is the principal source.

16, Durham Villas, Campden Hill. W.

The Toad scrambled to his feet, & scampered off down the road; & as he ran he heard the ferret laughing.

He went back & told the Water-rat. "What did I tell you?" said Rat.

Still, the Toad would not give in at once. He got a boat, & set off rowing up the river to the back of Toad Hall, to where the garden came down to the river side. All seemed very peaceful & deserted. As he rested on his oars he could see Toad Hall quiet in the sunshine, with the pigeons cooing on the roof, & the garden, & the creek that led to the boat-house, & the little wooden bridge that crossed it. He paddled up very cautiously & turned to go under the bridge, & was just passing it when

Crash!

A great stone, flung from the bridge,

16 Durham Villas, London
16 August 1907

Sometimes in the book, Grahame clogs the pace and spontaneity of the letters with over-elaborate detail. Thus Rat's last speech on this page becomes:

> 'If that is really so,' said the good-natured Rat, already appeased, 'then my advice to you is, considering the lateness of the hour, to sit down and have your supper, which will be on the table in a minute, and be very patient . . .'

smashed through the bottom of the boat, &
Toad found himself struggling in deep
water. He looked up, & saw two stoats
leaning over the bridge watching him.
"It'll be your head next time, Toads!"
said they. And as Toad swam to shore,
the stoats laughed & laughed & laughed,
till they nearly had two fits — that is,
one fit each, of course.

The Toad went back & told the Water
Rat. "What did I tell you?" said Ratty
crossly: "& look here! now you've been &
ruined my nice clothes that I lent you!"

Then the Toad was very humble, &
apologized to the Rat for getting his clothes
wet, & said " Ratty, I have been a
headstrong & a wilful Toad. Henceforward
I will be humble & submissive, & will do
nothing without your kind advice &
approval."

"If that is really so, said the Rat,
" then my advice is, to sit down & have
your supper & be patient. For I am

16 Durham Villas, London
16 August 1907

'Love is all very well in its way, but friendship is much higher', says the old Water-rat in Oscar Wilde's story *The Devoted Friend*, and Grahame's Rat, who also apparently 'is not a family man', echoes such sentiments. *The Wind in the Willows*, wrote Grahame, is 'clean of the clash of sex', but the pleasures of friendship are frequently celebrated. Perhaps Toad's cardinal error is that he repeatedly lets his friends down.

sure that we can do nothing until we have
seen the Mole & the Badger, & heard their news,
& taken their advice in the matter."

"Oho, the Mole & the Badger!" said the Toad
lightly: "Why, what's become of them? I had
forgotten all about them."

"Well may you ask" replied the Rat
reproachfully. "While you were riding about
in motor-cars, those two faithful animals
have been hiding in the wild-wood, living
living very rough & sleeping very hard, spying
& planning & contriving, how to get back
Toad Hall again for you. See what it is
to have true friends! Some day you'll be
sorry you didn't value them more while
you had got them."

So the Toad was humble & contrite
again, of course, & they sat down to
supper.

When they were about half-way
through, there came a knock at the door.
The Rat nodded mysteriously to the Toad,
& went to the door & opened it; & in
walked the Badger. His shoes were

Badger's underground stores.
An Arthur Rackham illustration for *The Wind in the Willows* (1940).

Badger and Mole are the 'animals' closest to Grahame himself. Like
Badger he was large and commanding, yet shy and awkward in society,
with a penchant for snoozing and hibernation. In the book Badger shares
Mole's enthusiasm for underground living:

> 'There's no security, or peace and tranquillity, except underground . . . No
> builders, no tradesmen, no remarks passed on you by fellows looking over
> your wall, and, above all, no *weather* . . . No, up and out of doors is good
> enough to roam about and get one's living in; but underground to come back
> to at last – that's my idea of *home*!'

covered with mud, & he looked very rough
& tousled; but then he was never a very
smart man, the Badger, at the best of
times. He shook Toad by the hand & said
"Welcome home Toad! Ah, what am I
saying? Home, indeed! This is a sad
meeting. Alas, poor, poor Toad!" Then he
sat down at the table & helped himself
to a large slice of cold pie.

The Toad was rather alarmed at this
sort of greeting; but the Rat nudged
him & whispered "Don't say anything.
He takes it very much to heart. And he's
always rather low when he's wanting
his victuals."

Presently there was another
knock. at The Rat nodded to the Toad,
& went to the door & ushered in
the Mole, very shabby & unwashed,
with bits of hay & straw sticking in
his fur.

(To be continued).

16 Durham Villas, London
21 August 1907

Grahame, though not liable 'to dance round' anybody, was like Mole in many respects. Both were headstrong and given to sudden impulses (*The Wind in the Willows* begins with such an impulse) and both could be tough when the situation required it, yet both were well aware of their limitations:

> 'The Mole saw clearly that he was an animal of tilled field and hedgerow, linked to the ploughed furrow, the frequented pasture, the lane of evening lingerings, the cultivated garden-plot. For others the asperities, the stubborn endurance, or the clash of actual conflict, that went with Nature in the rough; he must be wise, must keep to the pleasant places in which his lines were laid and which held adventure enough, in their way, to last for a lifetime.'

25

16, Durham Villas, Campden Hill. W.

21ˢᵗ Aug: 1907.

Dear Robinson

"Why, it's Toad!" cried the Mole,
his face brightening up. "Fancy seeing
you here!" And he began to dance round
him. "Thought you were locked up in
prison for the rest of your days! Why,
you must have managed to escape,
you clever Toad!"

The Rat pulled him by the arm, but
it was too late. The Toad was puffing
+ swelling already.

"Clever? Well, I'm cleverer than
you fellows seem to think me" said he.
"Of course I escaped. What's a prison to
me? But that's nothing to what I've
done since. Just let me tell you!"

"Well, well, said the Mole, moving
towards the table, "You can talk while
I eat. Not a bite since breakfast! O my,

16 Durham Villas, London
21 August 1907

In *The Wind in the Willows* Toad has 'paws', not 'hands'. While retaining their human personalities. Grahame is careful to make his characters convincingly animal.

O my!" And he sat down + helped himself
liberally to cold beef + pickles.

The Toad ~~straighten~~ straddled on
the hearth-rug, ~~&~~ thrust his hands into
his pockets, + pulled out a handful
of silver. "Look at that!" he said. "That's
not bad, for a few minutes work. And
how do you think I done it? Horse-dealing!
That's how I done it!"

"Go on, Toad!" said the Mole, immensely
interested.

"Toad, do be quiet, please," said
~~the~~ Rat: "and don't you egg him on,
Mole, ~~Mole got it~~ but please tell us
what the position is, + what's best to be
done".

- There isn't anything to be done, that
I can see" replied the Mole, grumpily. "It's
like the old riddle "Who goes round + round
the house + never inside the house?" The
Badger + I have been round + round the
house, night + day: always the same thing.
Sentries everywhere, guns poked out at
us, stones thrown at us: always an animal

on the look-out, and my! how they do laugh!
That's what annoys me most.'
 'It's very difficult' said the Rat,
reflecting deeply: 'But I think I see [in the depths of my mind] what
the Toad ought to do. He ought to _____'

16 Durham Villas, London
21 August 1907

In the book Badger has a 'thin' (not small) 'dry voice'. When writing it,
Grahame went through the letters with a fine-tooth comb and here, by the
change of a single adjective, suggests Badger's age and authority.

on the look-out, and my! how they do laugh!
That's what annoys me most."

"It's very difficult" said the Rat,
reflecting deeply: "But I think I see what _in the depths of my mind_
the Toad ought to do. He ought to ———"

"No, he oughtn't!" shouted the Mole,
with his mouth full. "Nothing of the sort.
He ought to ———

"Well, I shan't do it, any way" cried
the Toad, getting excited. "I'm not going
to be ordered about by you fellows. I'm
going to ———"

By this time they were all three talking
at once, at the top of their voices, & the
noise was simply deafening, when a small
dry voice said "Be quiet, all of you!"
and instantly everyone was silent.

It was the Badger, who had finished
his pie & turned round in his chair. When
he saw that they were all evidently waiting
for him to address them, he turned to the
table again & reached out for the cheese.

'There, there!' said the Badger, more
kindly, 'never mind. We're going to let
by-gones be by-gones. [and turn over a new leaf] But what the Mole
says is quite true. The Stoats are on
guard, & they're the best sentinels in the
world. No. It's no good our attacking the
place. They're too strong for us.'

And so great was the respect commanded
by the solid qualities of that admirable
animal, that not another word was
uttered till he had quite finished his
supper & brushed the crumbs from his
legs. The Toad fidgetted a bit, but
the Rat held him firmly down.

When the Badger had quite done, he
got up & stood before the fire, reflecting.
"Toad!" he said severely, "You're a bad
little animal! What would your father
have said, if he had been here tonight?"

The Toad began to shed tears, at once

"There, there!" said the Badger, more
kindly, "never mind. We're going to let
by-gones be by-gones. But what the Mole
says is quite true. The Stoats are on
guard, & they're the best sentinels in the
world. It's no good our attacking the
place. They're too strong for us."

"Then it's all over" sobbed the Toad, crying into
the sofa-cushions. "I shall go & enlist

for a soldier, and never see my dear Toad-Hall
any more!'

'Cheer up, Toady', said the Badger: 'Now
I'm going to tell you a secret.'

The Toad sat up at once & dried his eyes.
He liked to be told secrets, & then to go & tell
them to some other animal, after he had
promised not to.

'There – is – a – secret – passage' said
the Badger impressively, 'leading right into
the middle of Toad Hall!'

'O nonsense, Badger' said the Toad
rather airily: 'I know every inch of
Toad Hall, inside & out. Nothing of the
sort, I do assure you!'

'My young friend' said the Badger
severely, 'Your father, who was a very
worthy animal – much worthier than
some others I know – was a great friend
of mine. [and told me a deal he wouldn't have thought of telling you] He made that passage, in case
of danger, & when he had made it he showed

16 Durham Villas, London
21 August 1907

In the book, Toad's father 'discovered' the secret passage – 'he didn't make
it, of course; that was done hundreds of years before he ever came to live
here'. Elsewhere Grahame adds references to 'a conservatory' and a
'billiard room', thus emphasizing the age and grandeur of Toad's ancestral
home.

— 120 —

the [illegible] & [illegible] all ..[illegible]..
Toad [illegible]

16, Durham Villas, Campden Hill. W.

for a soldier, & never see my dear Toad-Hall
any more!"

"Cheer up, Toady", said the Badger; "now
I'm going to tell you a secret."

The Toad sat up at once & dried his eyes.
He liked to be told secrets, & then to go & tell
them to some other animal, after he had
promised not to.

"There - is - a - secret - passage" said
the Badger impressively, "leading right into
the middle of Toad Hall!"

"O nonsense, Badger" said the Toad
rather airily; "I know every inch of
Toad Hall, inside & out. Nothing of the
sort, I do assure you!"

"My young friend" said the Badger
severely, "Your father, who was a very
worthy animal - much worthier than
some others I know - was a great friend
of mine. He made that passage, in case
of danger, & when he had made it he showed

'Well, well' said he, 'perhaps I am
rather a talker. A popular like [such as]
[I am] me – my friends get round me – & then
I talk. Go on, Badger! How's this going
to help us?'

'Tomorrow night,' continued the Badger,
as I have found out by calling at the back-door
in [the] disguise [of a sweep], there is going to be a great
banquet. It's somebody's birthday – the
Head Weasel's, I believe. And the [weasels] animals
will be gathered in the dining-hall, feasting &
laughing & carrying on, & suspecting nothing.
No guns, no swords, no sticks, no arms of any
sort.'

'But the sentries will be posted, as usual'

16 Durham Villas, London
21 August 1907

Toad's acknowledgement that he is 'rather a talker' is expanded in the
book:

'... My friends get round me – we chaff, we sparkle, we tell witty stories –
and somehow my tongue gets wagging. I have the gift of conversation. I've
been told I ought to have a "salon", whatever that may be.'

Mouse, too, had a ready wit, and was once described as 'only a baby who
has swallowed a dictionary'. When Miss Stott, seeing that he needed a
new bootlace, said: 'Quick, take out the old one!', Mouse retorted: 'I
suppose, like the Devil, you have but a short time.' He divided grown-ups
into 'Goods' and 'No Goods' and one afternoon, when some people were
calling, 'was observed to run about the drawing-room with extraordinary
activity during the whole of their visit'. He later explained, 'I thought if I
kept moving I might escape being kissed.'

— 122 —

it to me. "Don't tell my son" said he. "He's

a good fellow, but he has a light character
& can't hold his tongue. If he is ever in a
real fix you may tell him, but not before!"

The other animals looked hard at
Toad, to see how he would take it. Toad
was inclined to be sulky at first. Then he
brightened up, being a good fellow.

"Well, well" said he, "perhaps I am
rather a talker. A popular fellow like
me — my friends get round me — & then
I talk. Go on, Badger! How's this going
to help us?"

"Tomorrow night," continued the Badger,
"as I have found out by calling at the back-door
in the disguise of a sweep, there is going to be a great
banquet. It's somebody's birthday — the
Head Weasel's, I believe. And the animals
will be gathered in the dining-hall, feasting &
laughing & carrying on, & suspecting nothing.
No guns, no swords, no sticks, no arms of any
sort."

"But the sentries will be posted, as usual"

remarked the rat.

'Exactly' said the Badger. [That is my point. The weasels] 'They will trust
entirely to [their excellent] the sentries. And that's where our passage
comes in. This blessed old passage [tunnel] leads right up
under the butler's pantry, next to the dining-hall!'

'Aha, that squeaky board in the butler's
pantry!' cried the Toad. 'Now I understand it'.

'– We shall creep out quietly into the butler's
pantry –' cried the Mole –

'– with our swords & our sticks & [our] things!' shouted
the Rat –

'– And rush in upon 'em! –' said the
Badger –

'And whack 'em, & whack 'em, and
whack 'em! –' cried the Toad in ecstasy,
running round & round the room &
jumping over the chairs.

'Very well then' said the Badger, becoming
suddenly grave & severe once more. Now that's
settled, all of you go off to bed, <u>at once</u>
& we'll make our arrangements [in the course of] tomorrow
[morning].

The Toad felt a great deal too
excited to sleep. But he had had a long

remarked the Rat.

"Exactly" said the Badger. "They will trust entirely to the sentries. And that's where our passage comes in. This blessed old passage leads right up under the butler's pantry, next to the dining-hall!"

"Aha, that squeaky board in the butler's pantry!" cried the Toad. "Now I understand it".

"— We shall creep out quietly into the butler's pantry —" cried the Mole —

"— with our swords and sticks & things!" shouted the Rat —

"— And rush in upon 'em! —" said the Badger —

"And whack 'em, & whack 'em, and whack 'em! —" cried the Toad in extasy, running round & round the room & jumping over the chairs.

"Very well then" said the Badger, becoming suddenly grave & severe once more. Now that's settled, all of you go off to bed, at once, & we'll make our arrangements tomorrow.

The Toad felt a great deal too excited to sleep. But he had had a long

He slept till a very late hour next
morning, & when he got down the other
animals had finished their breakfast
a long time. The Mole had gone out
by himself, without saying where he
was going to. The Badger sat in the
arm-chair, reading the paper & not troubling
himself in the slightest about what was
going to happen that evening. The Rat [on the other hand] was
running round excitedly with his arms full
of weapons, distributing them in four little
heaps, & saying rapidly under his breath, as he
ran, 'Here's-a-sword-for-the-Rat, here's-a-sword
for-the-Mole, here's-a-sword-for-the-Toad, here's-a-sword
for-the-Badger! Here's-a-pistol for the Rat, here's
a-pistol-for-the Mole,' & so on.

(To be continued)

16 Durham Villas, London
21 August 1907

Grahame's own dreams were often disturbing. In *Bertie's Escapade* (a
story written for Mouse, but not published until 1944) he described a
nightmare caused perhaps by his troubles at the Bank. He was at a great
City banquet and when the Chairman proposed the health of 'The King':

> 'he thought of a most excellent speech to make in reply . . . And he tried to
> make it, but they held him down in his chair and wouldn't let him. And then
> he dreamt that the Chairman actually proposed his own health . . . and he
> got up to reply, and he couldn't think of anything to say! And he stood there,
> for hours and hours it seemed, in a dead silence . . . Till at last the Chairman
> rose, "He can't think of anything to say! TURN HIM OUT!" '

& tiring day, & his head had not been long on the pillow before he was snoring. Of course he dreamt a great deal – such a jumble of gipsies, motor-cars & policemen, falling into water & fishing out again, as never was; & the secret passage twisted & turned, & shook itself, & sat up on its end; but somehow he was in Toad Hall at the ~~~~~ last, & his friends sat round him, saying what a clever Toad he was.

He slept till a very late hour next morning, & when he got down the other animals had finished their breakfast a long time. The Mole had gone out by himself, without saying where he was going to. The Badger sat in the arm-chair, reading the paper, & not troubling himself in the slightest about what was going to happen that evening. The Rat was running round excitedly with his arms full of weapons, distributing them in four little heaps, & saying rapidly under his breath, as he ran. "Here's-a-sword-for-the-Rat, here's-a-sword for-the-Mole, here's-a-sword-for-the-Toad, here's-a-swo for-the-Badger! Here's-a-pistol for the-Rat, here's-a-pistol-for-the-Mole," & so on.

(To be continued)

16 Durham Villas, London
26 August 1907

By now, Mouse has left Littlehampton and returned to Cookham Dene with Miss Stott. She later wrote that he had 'made friends everywhere'. He had learned to fish and to row, and 'when he said goodbye he took drawings as keepsakes for the man at the Ferry and for the boat man'.

29

16, Durham Villas, Campden Hill. W.

26th August, 1907.

Dear Robinson,

"That's all very well, Rat", said the Badger, looking at him over the edge of his newspaper. "I'm not blaming you. But let us just once get past those stoats, with their horrid guns, & I assure you we shan't want any swords or pistols. We four, with our sticks, once we're inside the dining-hall - why, we shall clear the floor of 'em, in five minutes. I'd have done the thing by myself, but I didn't want to deprive you fellows of the fun!"

"It's as well to be on the safe side" said the Rat, polishing a pistol-barrel on his sleeve & looking along it.

The Toad picked up a stout stick & swung it vigorously, throshing imaginary animals with it. "I'll learn 'em to steal my house"! he cried. "I'll learn 'em, I'll learn 'em!"

16 Durham Villas, London
26 August 1907

Badger's forbidding gruffness and curious mixture of pontification and poor grammar probably stem from the poet and journalist W. E. Henley. As editor of the *National Observer*, Henley was responsible for publishing most of Grahame's early essays and tried hard to persuade him to give up the Bank and become a full-time writer. Grahame, who maintained that he was a 'spring and not a pump', later wrote: 'Mr. Henley . . . took all I had and asked me for more: I should be a pig if I ever forgot him.'

"Don't say 'learn 'em', Toad", said the Rat, greatly shocked: "it's not good English!"

"What are you always nagging at Toad for?" enquired the Badger. "What's the matter with his English? It's the same what I use myself, & what's good enough for me ought to be good enough for you!"

"I'm sorry", said the Rat humbly: "Only I think it ought to be 'teach 'em', not 'learn 'em'."

"But we don't want to teach 'em" said the Badger. "We want to learn 'em, learn 'em, learn 'em! & what's more, we're going to!"

"O all right, have it your own way" said the Rat. He was getting rather muddled about it himself, & presently retired into a corner, where he was heard muttering 'learn 'em, teach 'em, teach 'em, learn 'em' — till the Badger told him

rather sharply to leave off.

Presently the Mole tumbled into the
room, evidently very pleased with himself.
"I've been humbugging the Stoats", he
began. "It was great fun. I put on
that old washerwoman-dress that Toad
came home in — found it hanging before
the kitchen fire — and the bonnet, &
went off to Toad Hall, & found the
Stoat-sentries with their guns at the
gate. "Good morning, gentlemen". I says.
"Want any washing done today"? They looked
at me very proud & haughty, & said "Go away
washerwoman! we don't do any washing
on duty!" "Or any other time?" says I!
"Haw, haw, haw! Wasn't I funny, Toad!"

"Poor, frivolous animal!" said the
Toad very loftily. The fact is, he was
jealous of Mole, for what he had done.
It was just what he would have liked
to do himself, if he had only thought of it.

"Some of the stoats turned quite pink"

'I could see them pricking up their ears'
went on Mole, 'My daughter' I said
'washes for Mr Badger, so I know what
I'm talking about. A hundred bloodthirsty
badgers, armed with rifles, are going to
attack tonight by way of the paddock.
Six boat-loads of rats, with pistols &
cutlasses, will come up the river &
effect a landing in the kitchen-garden;
& a picked body of Toads, known as the
Die-hards, or the Death-or-Glory Toads,
will storm the orchard. [yelling for vengeance. They seemed struck all of a heap.] Then I ran away
& hid: & presently I came creeping back
through the bushes. They were all as nervous
& excited as could be: running all
ways at once, & everyone giving different

16 Durham Villas, London
26 August 1907

The pencilled addition, 'yelling for vengeance', is included in the book,
while the vivid but colloquial, 'they seemed struck all of a heap', is
omitted.

continued the Mole: "and the Sergeant
said to me, very stiffly, "Now run away,
my good woman, run away!" "Run
away?" I said, "It won't be me that'll
be running away, in a very short time from
now!"

"O Moly!" said the Rat, dismayed.

The Badger laid down his paper.

"I could see them pricking up their ears"
went on Mole. "My daughter" I said
"washes for Mr Badger, so I know what
I'm talking about. A hundred bloodthirsty
badgers, armed with rifles, are going to
attack tonight by way of the paddock.
Six boat-loads of rats, with pistols &
cutlasses, will come up the river &
effect a landing in the kitchen-garden:
& a picked body of Toads, known as the
Die-hards, or the Death-or-Glory Toads,
will storm the orchard". Then I ran away
& hid: & presently I came creeping back
through the bushes. They were all as nervous
& excited as could be: running all
ways at once, & everyone giving different

16, Durham Villas, Campden Hill. W.

orders, & the Sergeant sending off bodies of stoats to distant parts of the grounds in different directions; and I heard one stoat say — "That's just like the weasels; they're to stop comfortably at home, & have feasting & all sorts of fun, & we're to stay out in the cold & the dark & be cut to pieces by bloodthirsty badgers!"

"You silly ass, Mole", cried the Toad. — "You've been & spoilt everything!"

"Mole", said the Badger, in his dry quiet way, "You have more sense in your little finger than some other animals have in the whole of their fat bodies. I begin to have great hopes of you. Good Mole! Clever Mole!"

The Toad was simply wild with jealousy, especially as he couldn't see what the Mole had done that was particularly clever; but before he could

say more the dinner-bell rang. It was
bacon & broad beans, & a macaroni
pudding; & when they had quite done,
the badger settled himself into an arm-
chair & said "Well, we've got our work
cut out for us tonight, & we shall be up
rather late, so I'm going to have forty
winks". And he drew a handkerchief
over his face & was soon snoring.

The Rat was still taken up with his
arrangements, ~~& began~~ continued running
between his four little heaps, muttering
"Here's-a-belt-for-the-Rat, here's-a-belt
for-the-Mole, here's-a-belt-for-the-Toad,
here's-a-belt-for-the-Badger", & so on,
so the Mole put his arm through the Toad's
& drew him into the garden, where he
put him into a wicker-chair & made him
tell him all his adventures from beginning
to end, which the Toad was very willing
to do. Indeed, he not only told him

16 Durham Villas, London
26 August 1907

Remembering the cautionary tale, Grahame is gently critical of Toad's
fabrications – but in the book he makes no such apology, adding:

> 'Much that he related belonged more properly to the category of what-
> might-have-happened-had-I-only-thought-of-it-in-time-instead-of-ten-
> minutes-afterwards. Those are always the best and the raciest adventures;
> and why should they not be truly ours, as much as the somewhat inadequate
> things that really come off?'

As Constance Smedley noted 'the brisk adventures . . . to please a child'
have become the framework for a 'maturer set of memories'.

everything, but I'm afraid he also told him several things that had not actually occurred; but they were all things that the Toad had intended to do, if he had had time: so perhaps he had almost persuaded himself that he had really done them.

When it grew dark, the Rat called them into the parlour, & stood each of them by his little heap, & proceeded to dress them up. He was very earnest about it & it took quite a long time. First there was a belt to go on each animal, & then a sword to be stuck into each belt, & then a cutlass on the other side to balance it, & then a pair of pistols, & a policeman's truncheon, & a pair of handcuffs, & some bandages & sticking-plaster, & a sandwich-case. The Badger laughed good-humouredly, & said "All right, Rat; it amuses you & it doesn't hurt me. But I'm going to do all I've got to do with this here stick!" But the Rat

'Now then, follow me.'
A Paul Branson illustration for *The Wind in the Willows* (1913).

said "Please, Badger! You know I shouldn't like you to blame me afterwards & say I had forgotten anything!"

When all was ready, the Badger ~~said~~ ~~took~~ took a dark lantern in his hand & said "Now then, follow me! Mole first, 'cos I'm very pleased with him: Rat next; Toad last. And look here, Toady! don't you chatter quite so much.

The Toad was so anxious to begin the attack that he took up the inferior position assigned to him without a murmur, & the animals set off. The Badger led them along by the river for some way, & then suddenly swung himself over the edge into a hole in the river-bank. The others followed silently one by one; of course when it came to the Toad's turn he managed to slip or fall into the water with a loud splash. He was hauled out by the others, & rubbed down, & comforted; but the Badger was seriously angry & told him that the next time he made a fool of himself he would be left behind. (To be cont?)

16 Durham Villas, London
7 September 1907

'And partly also because' is a rare example of a clumsy phrase, which Grahame corrects in the book. The quality of the letters is now such that whole passages are transcribed almost verbatim.

33

16, Durham Villas, Campden Hill. W.

7. Sept.^r ~~Oct.~~ 1907

Dear Robinson

So at last they were in the secret passage!

It was cold, & dark, & damp, & muddy, & low; & the Toad began to shiver with dread, & partly also because he was wet through; & he lagged behind, & the others called out impatiently "Come on, Toad!" Then he 'came on' with such a rush that he upset the Rat into the Mole & the Mole into the Badger. And the Badger thought they were attacked from behind, & drew a pistol, as there wasn't room to use a stick; & he nearly put a bullet through m^r. Toad. When he found out what had really happened he was very angry, & said "Now Toad shall be left

16 Durham Villas, London
7 September 1907

The 'scene' in the underground passage, like so much of the story, cries out for dramatization. Curtis Brown soon saw the theatrical possibilities in the book, but sent it to manager after manager without success. They thought it 'too whimsical' and 'quite impossible' to represent the animals in 'believable costumes'. Brown then thought of A. A. Milne, who was immediately enthusiastic, and wrote: 'When characters have been created as solidly as those of Rat, and Mole, Toad and Badger, the dramatist has merely to listen and record.' His *Toad of Toad Hall*, which had its first London production in 1930, began a theatrical life for the book which continues today.

behind this time!" But Toad whimpered,
& the other two promised they would be
answerable for him, & at last the Badger
was pacified & the Toad was allowed to
proceed, only this time the Rat brought
up the rear, with a firm grip on the
shoulder of Toad.

So they groped along & shuffled along,
with their paws on their pistols, & presently
the Badger said "We must be getting very
near the Hall now!" Then they heard, far
away & over their heads, a confused murmur
of sound, as if people were shouting & cheering
& stamping & hammering on tables; & the
Toad got nervous, but the Badger only
said "Well, they are going it, those Weasels!"

They groped along a bit further, & presently
the noise broke out again, quite distinct
this time, & close above them. "OO-ray-oo-
ray-oo-ray-oo-ray!" they heard, & the
stamping of little feet on the floor, & the
clinking of glasses as little paws hammered
on the table. "They are going it!" said the

34

Badger: "Come on!" And they hurried along the passage till they found themselves standing under the trap-door that led into the butler's pantry.

There was such a noise going on in the Hall that there was little danger of their being overheard. The Badger said "Now, all together!" and the four of them put their shoulders to the trap-door & heaved it back. In another second they all stood in the pantry, with only a door between them & the dining-hall!

For the moment the noise was simply deafening. As the cheering & hammering slowly subsided, a voice was heard, saying "Well, I will not detain you longer" (much applause) "But before I sit down" (great cheering) "I should like to say one word about our host Mr. Toad! We all know Toad! (laughter) Good Toad, honest Toad, modest Toad!" (Shrieks of merriment).

"Only let me get at him!" muttered Toad, grinding his teeth.

"Hold hard a minute" said the Badger, restraining him with difficulty.

"— Let me sing you a little song" went on the voice; "which I have composed on the

Well might the terrified weasels dive
under the tables & spring at the windows!
Well might the ferrets rush for the fire-
place & get jammed in the chimney!
Well might tables & chairs be upset &
glass & china sent smashing on the
floor, in the panic of that terrible
moment when the Four Heroes strode
wrathfully into the room! The
mighty Badger, his whiskers bristling,
his great cudgel whistling through

16 Durham Villas, London
7 September 1907

Peter Green, in his excellent critical biography, has noted the Homeric
motif in the story. Toad's exploits are a kind of comic *Odyssey*, and in the
last chapter, 'The Return of Ulysses', Grahame parodies the hero's return
and the slaying of the suitors.

subject of Toad!" (Much applause).

Then the head-weasel — for it was he — began in a high squeaky voice

"Toad he went a-pleasuring
Gaily down the street —"

The Badger drew himself up, took a firm grip of his stick in both hands, & cried

"The hour is come! Follow me!"
and flung the door open wide.

My!

What a squeaking & a squeaking & a screeching filled the air!

Well might the terrified weasels dive under the tables & spring at the windows! Well might the ferrets rush for the fire-place & get jammed in the chimney! Well might tables & chairs be upset & glass & china sent smashing on the floor, in the panic of that terrible moment when the Four Heroes strode wrathfully into the room! The mighty Badger, his whiskers bristling, his great cudgel whistling through

the air! Mole, black & grim & terrible,
brandishing his stick & shouting his
awful war-cry 'A Mole, A Mole!'
Rat, desperate & determined, his belt
bulging with weapons of every age &
every variety; Toad, frenzied with
excitement & injured pride, swollen to
twice his ordinary size, leaping into
the air & emitting Toad-whoops that
chilled [through] the marrow! 'Toad he went
a-pleasuring!' he yelled. 'I'll pleasure
'em!' [and he made straight for the Chief Weasel] They were but four, yet to the
panic-stricken weasels the hall seemed
full of monstrous animals, grey, black,
brown, & yellow, whooping & flourishing
enormous sticks; & they broke & fled
with squeals of terror, this way & that,
through the windows, up the chimney,
anywhere to get out of reach of those
terrible cudgels.

16, Durham Villas, Campden Hill. W.

the air! Mole, black & grim & terrible, brandishing his stick & shouting his awful war-cry "A Mole, A Mole!" Rat, desperate & determined, his belt bulging with weapons of every age & every variety; Toad, frenzied with excitement & injured pride, swollen to twice his ordinary size, leaping into the air & emitting Toad-whoops that chilled the marrow! "Toad he went a-pleasuring!" he yelled. "I'll pleasure 'em!" — as he went straight for the Chief Weasel. They were but four, yet to the panic-stricken weasels the hall seemed full of monstrous animals, grey, black, brown, & yellow, whooping & flourishing enormous sticks; & they broke & fled with squeals of terror, this way & that, through the windows, up the chimney, anywhere to get out of reach of those terrible cudgels.

16 Durham Villas, London
7 September 1907

Grahame's evident enjoyment of the defeat of the Wild Wooders may well reflect his strong conservative political views. Though Mouse, like Elspeth, was a Liberal (he threatened 'with fists' a woman who said that 'Gladstone was a wicked old man'), Grahame had a deep distrust of social change.

In 1906, the year before the letters were written, fifty-three Labour MPs entered Parliament, and before the next general election, Grahame wrote to Quiller-Couch, who was a staunch Liberal: 'I must not wish you luck in your nefarious designs on our savings, our cellars and our garden-plots.'

The affair was soon over. Up & down,
the length of the hall, strode the four
Animals, whacking with their sticks
at every head that showed itself.
In five minutes the room was cleared.
Through the broken windows by which
they had escaped the shrieks of terrified
weasels escaping across the lawn were
borne faintly to their ears; on the floor
lay some dozen or so of the enemy, on
whom the Mole was busily engaged
in fitting handcuffs. The Badger, resting
from his labours, leaned on his stick &
wiped his honest brow. "Mole!" he said,
"You're the best of fellows! Cut along
outside & look after those stoats of yours!
I've an idea we shan't have much trouble
from them tonight!"

The Mole vanished through a window;
& then the Badger bade the other two set
a table on its legs, & pick up some plates

The animals have huge appetites, and so did Grahame. As a young man he frequented the restaurants of Soho where 'about ten courses' cost 1s. 6d., and he loved Cornish food – 'licky' (leek) pasties and 'star-gazy' pie. He later wrote that in Marseilles once he ate, 'a perfectly whacking and stupendous quantity of bouillabaisse'. He adored Italian food, especially the ice-cream, and when in Rome the architecture played second fiddle to the cuisine. When ill-health finally forced him to diet, his constant cry was: '*Do* let me have something to eat!'

& glasses, & see if they could find materials for a supper. "I want some grub, I do," he said, in the rather common way he had of speaking: "Stir your stumps, Toad, & look lively. We're doing all this for you, & you don't trouble to produce so much as a sandwich!"

The Toad felt rather hurt that the Badger didn't say pleasant things to him, as he had to the Mole, & tell him what a fine fellow he was, & how splendidly he had fought; for he was rather particularly pleased with himself, & the way he had gone for the head weasel & sent him flying across the table with one blow of his stick; but he bustled about, & so did the others, & presently they found some guava jelly in a glass dish, a cold chicken, a tongue that had hardly been touched, some trifle, & quite a lot of lobster salad; & in the pantry was a basket-full of French rolls, & a quantity

of celery & cheese. They were just sitting down when the Mole clambered in through the window chuckling, his arms full of rifles.

"It's all over" he said. "When the stoats heard the shrieks & the yells & the uproar inside the hall, most of them threw down their rifles & fled. The rest stood fast, but when the weasels rushed out upon them they thought they were betrayed, & the stoats grappled with the weasels, & the weasels fought to get away, & they wrestled & wriggled & rolled till they fell into the river! And I've got all their rifles, so that's all right."

"Excellent animal" said the Badger, his mouth full of chicken & trifle: "now there's just one more thing I want you to do for us, Mole, before you sit down to your supper along of us: because I can trust you to see a thing through, & I wish I could say the same of everybody I know."

(To be cont^d)

16 Durham Villas, London
September 1907

This wholesome, ordered world of 'clean linen', well-made beds and well-stocked larders is at odds with the Grahames' own eccentric later life style. Eighteen months after the book was published they moved to Blewbury, on the edge of the Berkshire downs, where they lived, by Grahame's own admission, 'in a state of primitive simplicity, which is almost shocking'. It was reported that mice were nesting in the larder and that Elspeth, who often went to bed in her clothes, put her husband into special underwear, which he changed only once a year.

37

16. Durham Villas
Kensington
Sept 1907.

Dear Robinson

"What I want you to do, Mole,"
said the Badger, "is to take those fellows
on the floor there, upstairs with you, & have
some bedrooms cleaned out, & tidied, & made
really comfortable. Make them put clean
linen on all the beds, & turn down
one corner of the bedclothes, just as you
know it ought to be done; & have a can
of hot water & clean towels put in
each room; & then you can give them
a licking apiece, if you've a mind
to, & put them outside the door — they
won't trouble us any further, I'll lay.
And then come in & have some of this
cold tongue. It's real good. I'm very
pleased with you, Mole!"

Then the Mole pulled his chair
to the table & pitched into the cold
tongue: & the Toad [like the gentleman he was] with an effort put
aside all his jealousy, and said heartily

So the goodnatured Mole formed his prisoners up in a line on the floor, & said "Quick, march!" & marched them off to the bedrooms; & presently he came down smiling, & said every room was ready, & as clean as a new pin. "And I didn't have to lick them either," he added. "I thought they had had licking enough for one night, & the weasels, when I put it to them, quite agreed with me. And they were very sorry & very penitent, & said it was all the fault of the head-weasel & the stoats, & if ever they could do anything for us at any time — & so on. So I gave them a roll apiece & let them out at the back door, & off they ran!"

Then the Mole pulled his chair to the table & pitched into the cold tongue; & the Toad with an effort put aside all his jealousy, & said heartily

'Mole, you're a brick, & a clever brick! [Thank you kindly, dear Mole, for all that you have]
[done for me today] I wish I had your headpiece!' The
Badger was pleased at that, & said
'Good old [There spoke my brave] toad!' So they finished
their supper in great joy & contentment,
& presently retired to rest, between clean
sheets, in the ancestral home of Toad,
which they had won back by
their valour [their strategy] and their sticks.

16 Durham Villas, London
September 1907

Grahame was a meticulous prose stylist, speaking once of 'the pleasurable agony of attempting stately sentences'. Believing that language was written for the ear, he balanced words with musical precision. Thus in the book, Toad's ancestral home is, 'won back by matchless valour, consummate strategy, and a proper handling of sticks.'

38

Mole, you're a brick, & a clever brick! I wish I had your headpiece!" The Badger was pleased at that, & said 'Good old Toad!" So they finished their supper in great joy & contentment, & presently retired to rest, between clean sheets, in the ancestral home of Toad, which they had won back ~~fashion~~ by their valour, their strategy, & their sticks.

Next morning the Toad, who had overslept himself, came down to breakfast disgracefully late, & found a certain quantity of eggshells on the table, some fragments of cold toast, a coffee-pot two-thirds empty, & really very little else; which did not tend to improve his temper, considering that after all it was his own house. The Mole & the Water-Rat were sitting in

wicker-chairs out on the lawn,
telling each other stories; roaring with
laughter & kicking their short legs up in
the air. The Badger, who was deep in
the morning paper, merely looked up &
nodded when the Toad came in. But
the Toad knew his man, so he sat down
& made the best breakfast he could,
observing to himself that he would get
square with the others, sooner or later.

When he had nearly finished the Badger
remarked rather shortly: "I'm afraid
there's a heavy morning's work in front
of you, Toad; you see we ought to have
a Banquet, to celebrate this affair!"

"O, all right," said the Toad, readily.
"anything to oblige. though Why on earth
you should want to have a Banquet in
the morning I cannot understand. But
you know I do not live to please myself,

16 Durham Villas, London
September 1907

After resigning from the Bank and moving to Blewbury, Grahame became increasingly indolent. He wrote 'any quantity of magnificent letters' in his armchair, 'with closed eyes', or 'strolling in the woods – or with head on pillow very late on a thoroughly wet and disagreeable morning.' But rarely were they written down and sent.

but only to give ~~pleasure~~ satisfaction to my friends, & do
everything they want,
∧ "for dear Badger!"

"Don't pretend to be stupider than you
are" said the Badger crossly; & don't chuckle
& splutter in your coffee when you're talking.
It's rude. What I mean is, the Banquet
will be at night, of course, but the
invitations have got to go out at once,
and you've got to write 'em! Now sit
down at that table — there's stacks of
paper on it, with "Toad Hall" at the
top in blue & gold — & write to all
your friends, & perhaps if you stick
to it you'll have done by lunch time.
And I'll help you, too. I'll order the
Banquet!"

"What!" cried the Toad, dismayed:
"me write a lot of rotten letters on a
jolly morning like this, when I want
to go round my property, & set everything
& everybody to rights, & enjoy myself!

I'll be — I'll see you — stop a minute though! Why, certainly, dear Badger! What is my pleasure or convenience to that of others? You wish it done & it shall be done. Go, my dear Badger, join our young friends outside in their innocent amusements. I sacrifice this fair morning on the altar of duty & friendship!"

The Badger looked at him very suspiciously, but Toad's frank open countenance made it difficult to suggest any unworthy motive in this change of attitude. As soon as the door had closed behind the Badger, the Toad hurried to the writing-table. He had had a fine idea while he was talking. He would write the invitations, to the otter, & all the hedgehogs, & the squirrels, & all the rest of them; & he would work in, somehow, what he had done during

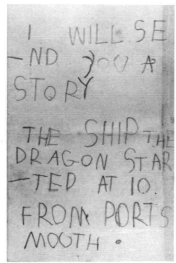

Extract from a story
by Alastair Grahame.

Toad's egocentric pretensions may well be a gentle satire of Mouse. Before he could read or write, Mouse had, according to Elspeth, 'imagined' a three-act play called *Beauty Born*, and 'dictated it with all the Acts, Scenes, Characters and other instructions'. He loved dressing-up and later announced in a letter from Littlehampton: 'I have made a vow that i will run away to the Stage !!! as soon as i can !!! help!' He also 'edited' a nursery magazine, *The Merry Thought*, to which Grahame contributed the short piece, *Bertie's Escapade*, about the Grahames' pig, who goes carol singing. Meanwhile Mouse, encouraged presumably by Elspeth, sang of love:

SONG OF MOUSE THIS MORNING

I must leave you my sweetest lover,
I go to take a wife
To lead another life
Tuleroo Tuleroo Tuleroo
But soon I will come back
Tuleroo Tuleroo.

the fight, & how he had laid the head-weasel
flat; & the invitation-cards should have
a note at the foot, something like this:

SPEECH . . . . by Toad
(There will be other speeches by Toad
during the evening.)

SONG . . . . . by Toad
(composed by himself.)

Other Compositions . . . by Toad
will be sung at intervals . . . by the Composer.

—————

The idea pleased him mightily, &
he worked hard & got the letters finished
by lunch-time, when it was reported
that there was a small & rather
bedraggled weasel at the door, enquiring
timidly whether he could be of any
service to the gentlemen. The Toad
went out, & found it was one of the

handcuffed ones of the previous evening,
very timid & very respectful. Toad
patted him on the head, shoved the
invitations into his paw, & told him
to deliver them all at once, & if he would
come back the next day perhaps there
might be a shilling for him & perhaps
there mightn't; & the poor weasel seemed
really quite grateful, & hurried off
eagerly to do his mission.

The other animals came in to lunch
very boisterous & happy, after a morning's
boating on the river, & expecting to find
Toad somewhat sulky & depressed.
Instead, he was so uppish & inflated
that of course they began to suspect
something; & the Rat & the Badger
exchanged significant glances.

After the meal was over the Toad thrust
his hands deep into his trouser-pockets,
& was swaggering off into the garden, where
he wanted to think out a few ideas for his
speeches, when the Rat caught him by the arm.

16 Durham Villas, London
September 1907

The final letter, like the previous one, is neither written on headed notepaper nor precisely dated. Perhaps Grahame, eager to finish the story, wrote them at a sitting, but sent them to Mouse separately. And so he finished the sequence, writing primarily, not for Mouse, nor even for 'Robinson', but for himself.

16 Durham Villas, Kensington

Sept 1907.

Dear Robinson

The Toad rather suspected
what he was after, & did his best
to get away; but the Badger taking
him firmly by the other arm, he
saw that the game was up. The
animals conducted him between them
into the small smoking-room that
opened out of the entrance-hall, shut
the door & put him down into a chair.
Then they stood in the front of him, while
the Toad sat silent & looked at them
with much suspicion & ill-humour.

"Now look here, Toad," said the
Rat: "about this Banquet. We
want you to understand, once & for
all; there must be no speeches, and
no songs. We're not arguing with
you; we're just telling you."

16 Durham Villas, London
September 1907

Mouse, too, loved singing. At Littlehampton he enjoyed, 'the lively songs of Mr. Fred Spencer of Dan Randall's old company and sang cheerfully in a children's competition:

> Always wear a flower in your coat,
> When you go to meet your girl.'

Some of the songs were clearly less innocent, and his parents shared Rat's disapproval. In a later letter Mouse assured them: 'We hear no vulgar songs.'

The Toad saw he was trapped. They understood him, they saw through him, they got ahead of him. His pleasant dream was shattered.

"Mayn't I sing them just one little song?" he said piteously.

"No, not one little song" said the Rat firmly, though his heart bled as he noticed the trembling lip of the poor disappointed Toad. "It's no good, Toady; you know your songs are all conceit & boasting, & vanity; & your speeches are all self-praise and - and - gross exaggeration and - and -"

"and gas" put in the Badger, in his common way.

"It's for your own good, Toady", went on the Rat. "You must turn over a new leaf, & now seems a

splendid time to begin. Don't think
that saying this doesn't hurt me
more than it hurts you!"

The Toad remained a long while
plunged in thought; at last he raised
his head, & the traces of strong emotion
were visible on his features. "You have
conquered, my friends!" he said. "It
was but a small thing that I asked—
merely leave to "blow" for yet one more
evening, to let myself go & hear the
tumultuous applause which always
seems to me—somehow—to bring
out my best qualities! But you
are right, I know, & I am wrong.
Henceforth I will be an altered toad.
My friends, you shall never have
occasion to blush for me again.
But, O dear O dear, this is a <u>hard</u>

world!'

And, pressing his handkerchief to his
face, he left the room with faltering
footsteps.

'Badger', said the Rat. 'I feel
like a brute; what do you feel like?

'O I know, I know,' said Badger:
but the thing's got to be done. This
dear good fellow has got to live here:
do you want him to be mocked, and
scorned [jeered], & laughed at, by stoats &
weasels?'

[No of course not said the Rat] 'Talking of weasels' said the Rat, 'It's
lucky we came upon that little weasel
just as he was setting out with Toad's
invitations. I confiscated the lot,

16 Durham Villas, London
September 1907

There is harshness and pathos, as Toad is compelled to turn over a new
leaf. Grahame had already realized the satirical potential of the animal
fable, writing in his introduction to *A Hundred Fables of Aesop*: 'The
friendly, tactful, unobtrusive beasts . . . could they not be seized upon and
utilised to point the requisite moral?'

The moral in this case is not simply that the self-willed child must be
restrained for the good of himself and society. The story is also perhaps, at
a deeper level, the cry of the repressed hedonist, who in his fantasy allows
his instincts to run wild, only to demonstrate, as much to himself as to
others, how vital it is that reckless self-expression be reined in.

world!"

And, pressing his handkerchief to his face, he left the room with faltering footsteps.

"Badger", said the Rat, "I feel like a brute; what do you feel like?"

"O I know, I know," said Badger; but the thing's got to be done. This dear good fellow has got to live here; do you want him to be mocked, & scorned, & laughed at, by stoats & weasels?"

"~~I am somehow missing the Rat mournfully; but he won't look half such a speals co respond when you can speak to him~~"

"Talking of weasels" said the Rat, "it's lucky we came upon that little weasel first as he was setting out with Toad's invitations. I confiscated the lot,

16 Durham Villas, London
September 1907

Toad, the extrovert, gives his final performance for himself alone, discovering the self-reliance of the imaginative child. Mouse, according to Constance Smedley, 'had a land of imaginary men, whom he captained', and 'crawled about beneath the table, which was a mountain pass, or mounted the chairs in desperate adventures'. Miss Stott wrote that, 'he lived a great deal in an imaginary world of his own making', and called it, 'Puppyland, where it is never silly to be silly'.

and the good Mole is now sitting in the
blue boudoir, filling up plain simple
invitation-cards." .   .   .   .   .
.   .   .   .
.   .   .   , ...

When at last the hour for the
banquet began to draw near,
Toad slipped away from the others
+ went upstairs to his own bedroom
very melancholy + thoughtful. Sitting
down in an armchair he rested his
brow upon his hand + pondered long.
Gradually his countenance cleared, + he
began to smile long slow smiles; then
he took to giggling in a shy, self conscious
manner. Then he got up, locked the
door, drew the curtains across the
windows, took all the chairs in
the room + arranged them in a
semi-circle, + took up his position

16 Durham Villas, London
September 1907

In the book, Grahame allows us to savour Toad's last great moment:

'Then he bowed, coughed twice, and, letting himself go, with uplifted voice
he sang, to the enraptured audience that his imagination so clearly saw.'

in front of them, swelling visibly.
Then he lifted his voice &, letting himself
go, sang loudly

Toad's last little Song!

" The Toad — came — home!
" There was panic in the parlours and
           howling in the halls,
" There was crying in the cowsheds &
           shrieking in the stalls,
" When the Toad — came — home!

" When the Toad — came — home!
" There was smashing in of windows and
           cracking in of doors,
" There was chivvying of weasels that
           fainted on the floor,
" When the Toad — came — home!

" Bang go the drums!
" The trumpeters are tooting & the soldiers
           are saluting
" And the cannon they are shooting and
         the — motor cars are hooting
" As the Hero comes!

'Shout-Hoo-ray!
'And let each one of the crowd [try &] do his
    best to shout it [very] <u>loud</u>,
'In honour of an animal of whom
    you're rightly [justly] proud,
'For it's Toad's great day!'

"Shout – Hoo–ray!

"And let each one of the crowd do his
                    best to shout it loud,

'In honour of an animal of whom
                    you're rightly proud,

"For its Toad's great day!"

He sang it, as has been said, very
loud; also, he sang it over twice.

Then he heaved a deep sigh; a
long, long, long sigh.

Then he dipped his hair-brush
in the water-jug, parted his hair in
the middle, & plastered it down very
straight & sleek on each side; and,
unlocking the door, went quietly down
the stairs to greet his guests, who were
assembling in the drawing-room.

Everyone shouted when he entered,
& crowded round him to congratulate
him & say nice things about his courage,

16 Durham Villas, London
September 1907

When asked what became of Toad's good resolutions, Grahame wrote: 'Of course Toad never really reformed; he was by nature incapable of it. But the subject is a painful one to pursue.'

When A. A. Milne demanded a sequel, 'a second wind', Grahame replied: 'Sequels are often traps which the wise author does well to avoid, if he wants to go, like Christian, on his way singing!'

& his cleverness, & his fighting qualities;
but Toad only smiled faintly & murmured
" Not at all, not at all!" or sometimes
" On the contrary!" The animals were
evidently quite puzzled & taken aback
by this new attitude of his; & Toad
felt, as he moved from one guest to
another, making his modest responses,
that he was an object of absorbing
interest to everyone.

The Badger had ordered everything of the
best, & the banquet was a great success.
There was much talking, & laughter, &
chaff, but through it all the Toad, who
was in the Chair, looked down his
nose & murmured pleasant nothings
to the animals on each side of him.
At intervals he stole a glance at the
Badger & the Rat, & saw them looking
at each other with their mouths open;
& this gave him the greatest satisfaction.